That Futebol Feeling

David Faflik

That Futebol Feeling

Sport and Play in Brazil's Heartland

TEMPLE UNIVERSITY PRESS
Philadelphia / Rome / Tokyo

TEMPLE UNIVERSITY PRESS
Philadelphia, Pennsylvania 19122
tupress.temple.edu

Library of Congress Cataloging-in-Publication Data

Names: Faflik, David, 1972– author.
Title: That futebol feeling : sport and play in Brazil's heartland / David
   Faflik.
Description: Philadelphia : Temple University Press, 2025. | Includes
   bibliographical references and index. | Summary: "This book examines the
   relationship between futebol team Clube Atlético Mineiro and its
   supporters in the Minas Gerais region of Brazil. The author reflects on
   the similarities and differences between the meanings of play in South
   American and North American contexts. The book interviews stakeholders
   during times of national crisis"— Provided by publisher.
Identifiers: LCCN 2024025590 (print) | LCCN 2024025591 (ebook) | ISBN
   9781439926048 (cloth) | ISBN 9781439926055 (paperback) | ISBN
   9781439926062 (pdf)
Subjects: LCSH: Clube Atlético Mineiro—Case studies. | Soccer—Social
   aspects—Brazil—Minas Gerais. | Soccer players—Brazil—Minas Gerais. |
   Soccer fans—Brazil—Minas Gerais. | COVID-19 Pandemic, 2020—Social
   aspects—Brazil—Minas Gerais.
Classification: LCC GV943.6.C564 F34 2025 (print) | LCC GV943.6.C564
   (ebook) | DDC 796.334/63098151—dc23/eng/20241121
LC record available at https://lccn.loc.gov/2024025590
LC ebook record available at https://lccn.loc.gov/2024025591

9 8 7 6 5 4 3 2 1

. . . for Grant Farred,

writer, teacher, thinker, friend

Contents

List of Illustrations

Acknowledgments

I begin these acknowledgments by thanking an entire city and state, Belo Horizonte, Brazil, in Minas Gerais state. Whatever inspiration I've had in writing this book has derived in no small part from the place and the people who provided me with a home during my four-month residence in Brazil. I am grateful to my hosts, without whom this book could not have taken shape.

I am equally indebted to the Fulbright Commissions of the United States and of Brazil for making my visit to the latter country possible. As a Fulbright Distinguished Chair in Studies of the United States at the Universidade Federal de Minas Gerais (UFMG), I spent the months between May and September 2022 teaching and researching in Belo Horizonte, where I wrote most of this book. To say that my Fulbright experience has been life-changing would be an understatement. It has been life-making, and I realize how fortunate I am to have had the opportunity to participate in a program that has given so much to so many. The faculty and staff at UFMG similarly befriended me after I arrived as a visitor in a place where I otherwise knew no one before the beginning of my stay. I left Belo Horizonte with more friends than I had when I started my residence, which means, in my estimation, that my trip was a success. Although I mention several individual UFMG faculty members by name in the following pages, I want to single out two of them here, Elcio Loureiro Cornelsen and Marcelino Rodrigues da Silva, for their kindness and their guidance into the scholarship on Brazilian *futebol*. Ricardo Fabrino Mendonça and Lucas Rezende were equally helpful as I learned to navigate my way around my host university. Dawisson Belém Lopes made my stay at UFMG even possible. And the students in the courses I taught at UFMG made my time in Belo Horizonte an absolute joy. From my undergraduate course, I want to thank Ane Caroline, Anderson Faleiro, Lucas Fernandes, Leonardo Franco, Aline Lopes, and Rafael de Azevedo Silva for inviting me to think about American literature and culture in new ways. And when I look back on my graduate seminar in "American Politics and Literature," I cannot help but smile when I remember how much edifying classroom fun we had. Thank you, Fernanda Guimarães, Luiz Silva, Henrique Gomes, Leandro Adriano, Túlio Ribeiro, Bruno Magalhães, Eduardo Vidal, Maria Rafaela, and Emanuella Ribeiro. Luiz, Leandro, and Eduardo will know what I mean when I say how grateful I am to them for joining me in thinking about Bartleby and other "problems."

At the heart of this book are the people whom I interviewed to learn more about the culture of Clube Atlético Mineiro, the top-flight Brazilian football team that constitutes the focal point of my study. These people all make their due appearances in this book, and I want to thank them here for taking the time and trouble to talk with a well-intentioned stranger from the United States. Without their insights, I could not have completed this project. I extend a sincere thank you, and *um grande abraço*, to the following *atleticanos*: Frederico Bolivar, Ricardo Galuppo, Rodolfo Gropen, Carol Leandro, João Leite, Márcio de Lima Leite, Helvécio Marins Jr., Rafael Miranda, Nelinho, Heleno Oliveira, Fred Melo Paiva, Paulo Roberto Prestes, Reinaldo, Réver, Alice Quintão Soares, and Victor. I have heard many people describe Clube Atlético Mineiro as a family. It is that, and one that made me feel most welcome during my time in Minas Gerais. To that end, I must also thank an additional member of this family, Emmerson Maurílio, the founder and president of the Centro Atleticano de Memória. No one knows more about Atlético Mineiro than Emmerson, and I have benefited greatly from his sharing his knowledge with me. Another colleague of mine at UFMG likewise resides in this family: The assistance that *atleti-cana* Luciana Fiuza offered during interviews as a translator, planner, and occasional coconspirator was invaluable in the completion of this book. Ryan Mulligan, my editor at Temple University Press, might not realize that he's also now an *atleticano*, at least in my eyes. I thank him, too. Note that the individuals who spoke with me on the record in support of this project did so on their own behalf, not as representatives or spokespersons for Clube Atlético Mineiro or any other group or organization. With gratitude, I should also note that funding from the University of Rhode Island's Center for the Humanities aided a portion of the preliminary research for this book as well as its preparation for publication.

My family back in the United States has sustained me from the very beginning, and I owe them everything for making life and love and work and play even possible. My mom and dad, Nan and Jim Faflik, have only ever encouraged their elder son. And my sister and brother, Julie and Jonathan Faflik, have been my first and best friends in all things. That I have been surrounded by such love has made all the difference.

That Futebol Feeling

1

Pre-match

> Both in and out of the game, and watching and
> wondering at it.
>
> —WALT WHITMAN, *Leaves of Grass* (1855)

This book records my own recent encounters as a fan with the
meanings of sport and play during what I'd rather ungram-
matically call "crisis times." At a moment when some seven million people worldwide have been lost to the ravages of the "novel"
SARS-CoV-2 coronavirus (COVID-19), the most recent in a spate
of viral pathogens to afflict populations across the globe, a fortunate group of survivors remains steadfast in its dedication to
playing and watching the games that pass somewhat misleadingly
under the catch-all label of "sport." Anthropologists characterize
sports and games as a nonpurposive form of leisure activity, in
which the participants obey a mutually agreed-upon set of regulations in their performance of rituals that combine seriousness with
entertainment, structure with spontaneity. By contrast, scholars
whose well-drilled conceptualizations of sport may have left them
with little inclination to indulge in "fun" view play as an open-
ended mode of human and animal behavior that's organized, or
not, according to the needs of its partakers in their pursuit of joyful pleasures that even the adults among them don't always understand.[1] This book addresses a curious reality about the games we
play in the twenty-first century: Neither the casualties associated
with a deadly disease, the disciplinary conditioning of academ-

ics (like me) who study sport, nor the great strains placed upon communities and shared local identities amid the fallout from the COVID-19 pandemic have spoiled our willingness to *play*, even in the wake of the dislocations we've sustained to our personal and political lives since late in the calendar year 2019.[2]

The world's continuing enthusiasm for "football" is conspicuous in this respect. Given its status as the planet's spectator sport of choice, the professional version of a recreational pastime that's also known as *futebol, fútbol, fußball, goru,* and *soccer* was among the earliest of games that contemporaries play to resume organized, televised competition in the late spring of 2020. Those of us with an emotional stake in the game will remember this as a time when leagues across Europe, Asia, and North and South America began to allow players to return to the pitch, with or without supporters in the stands. Public health authorities, meanwhile, urged the necessity of social distancing as a means of slowing COVID-19's harmful spread.

Football's rampant international commercialization over the last few decades may have made it something other than the improvised art form that fans have admired worldwide since the beginning of the previous century, long before aficionados mostly outside Brazil came to express their appreciation for the elevated standard of the sport they believed was played there by calling it the "beautiful game," or *jogo bonito*.[3] Football nevertheless retains its outsized popularity in- and outside Brazil. This favor is true notwithstanding the havoc COVID-19 has caused, and despite the fact that it's arguably harder now than ever before to distinguish between a supporter's attachments to his team and a consumer's expressions of purchased satisfaction.[4] Indeed, Brazil's own state football championships, which annually anticipate the start of the national domestic football league, the Campeonato Brasileiro Série A, or Brasileirão, were in the vanguard of competitions to restart during a global pandemic that showed no signs of abating. On a Thursday night in Rio de Janeiro, June 18, 2020, perennial favorites Flamengo beat Bangu 3–0 at the legendary Maracanã Stadium to kick off a new season of the regional Campeonato Carioca. At the time, Rio state had already suffered more than 8,500 fatalities from COVID-19. Nationwide, Brazil surpassed one million diagnosed cases of the disease on June 19, a total that then ranked the country second highest in the world behind only the United States. Regardless of these worrying signs, the games would continue to be played until Rio de Janeiro's mayor, Marcelo Crivella, suspended the state league just three days after it began, causing the resumption of play in surrounding states to stutter as a result. Still, come the early weeks of August 2020, when the domestic death toll from COVID-19 had climbed past one hundred thousand, the Brasileirão competition itself was set to get underway as debate raged in Brazil over the wisdom of reopening when so much more than just a game was at stake.[5]

The interrelated vagaries of life, love, and sport have never been the exclusive preserve of such storied capitals of world football as Brazil's two largest cities, Rio de Janeiro and São Paulo. The fervor and the fear attending football's version of the collective return to "normalcy" under the coronavirus have, in fact, been felt throughout each of Brazil's twenty-six states, including the state of Minas Gerais. Occupying a landmass larger than France in Brazil's southeastern interior, Minas Gerais might lack the postcard appeal of the country's heralded beaches, just as Brazilians' habit of associating the state with an idealized rural simplicity has denied it a certain cosmopolitan sophistication in the popular imagination. But *mineiros*, as those who are born and raised in Minas Gerais are known, reside in an area that Brazilians by and large regard with a special affection reserved for what many of them identify as the country's heartland. Not a few of the original settlers in the area from the seventeenth and eighteenth centuries are remembered today as a salt-of-the-earth assemblage of miners, farmers, ranchers, laborers, and merchants. Mineiros are furthermore a diverse people, representative of the demographic complexity that characterizes modern-day Brazil. That is, they are the descendants of the former slaves, free Blacks, colonial Portuguese, and indigenous groups who together have lent Brazil a richly variegated ethnic and cultural heritage. One of the aims of this book is to examine that heritage from the perspective of sport, using one state's provincial footballing tradition as the occasion to reconsider what allows life to persist in the face of the "new ideas, new structurations, and new understandings of what it means to be alive" that condition the realities of what David L. Andrews, Holly Thorpe, and Joshua I. Newman have described as "Sport and Physical Culture in Global Pandemic Times."[6] With that said, whether mineiros' enthrallment with football should be included among what ethnographers would adduce as the region's general defining features is a subject that lies beyond the scope of my own journalistic immersion in futebol, which is no more intended to be a conventional scholarly study of people's playful behaviors than it is an exceptionalist celebration of Brazilians' passionate regard for a sport that other nations care about just as much as they do. What my own fresh impressions do address is how the human determination to play (including with language, as the calculated wordplay in this study suggests) finds expression through sport in the best and worst of times, before and after COVID-19, and with a distinctive regional flair that noticeably distinguishes the local cultural meanings of futebol in one corner of Latin America from another.[7] To that end, I have written *That Futebol Feeling* knowing full well that scholars are only now beginning to seriously reconsider play per se after years of comparative neglect.[8] Some of them may object to the idiosyncratic nature of my subject matter, the local associations of which perhaps beg the question of significance as much as they do representation. Others could find fault with my method, which is informed as much by my creative response to having *been* there (that is, in Brazil) as it is the "science" of sociology or the kind of coolly unemotional data analysis that now guides the most efficient sports franchises.[9] Readers can refer to this volume's appendix to learn more about the decisions of style and method that I've made in completing a project that not only takes play as its primary topic but *plays* with that topic in ways that are intended to change how fans like us engage with the sports we love.

That Futebol Feeling consists of a series of selective profiles of the "players" who have recently plied their footballing trades with or in the emotional vicinity of Clube Atlético Mineiro (CAM). As a rule—all games have rules—these profiles are sometimes personal, never hagiographical, and always rhetorical, in the sense that this book argues that we can't begin to take the full measure of football until we take seriously the individual feelings of its participants.[10] Dutch social theorist Johan Huizinga, writing before the Second World War, concluded that modern sport was already "stiffening into seriousness but still being felt as play."[11] I have tried to resist a similar slide into a rigidity best described as unfun: first, by grounding this revisionist examination of sport at the grass roots, as it were, the better to avoid reducing Brazilians' feelings about football to a pervasive cultural condition; and second, by making a conscientious effort to balance the scholar's imperative to intellectualize with the instincts of players and fans to personalize the games we play. My interest, then, is in providing a playfully meditative, chronicle-style account of the emotions that football inspires among a given people in a specific place at a particular time.[12] Here, the focus is with the COVID-era players and supporters of the Belo Horizonte outfit Atlético Mineiro. I hesitate to offer a grand theory of Latin American affect with this project;[13] what I have written is a micro-history of the emotions, the better to address how play feels at a cultural moment when so many of us are working, dying, or both.

What I likewise need to stress at the start of this volume is that I have not chosen "Atlético," as the team is colloquially known, as a topic for consideration because of any special sporting prowess it might possess. The team does enjoy a regional pride of place in Minas Gerais state, with deference to the supporters of rival club sides Cruzeiro and the newly relegated América-MG. Its forty-eight Campeonato Mineiro titles form a record that no other regional side can match. League officials in Brazil may have just recognized in August 2023 CAM's pretensions to the title for the interstate Tournament of Champions, from 1937.[14] Yet until these past few years, Atlético had not amassed much hardware outside its home state since the Brasileirão launched as a nationwide football competition in 1971. The team coincidentally claimed this inaugural competition. But, only by the end of the Brasileirão's 2021 season, fifty years after the first, would Atlético once more finish atop the league standings, having placed as runners-up on five previous occasions. One could say that COVID has been kind to Atlético Mineiro in this respect; it won the 2021 editions of the Campeonato Mineiro and the Copa do Brasil, too, completing a domestic treble under the since-departed (professionally speaking) and later-reinstalled manager Cuca, even while the Brazilian casualties from COVID-19 mounted.[15] Atlético, in short, is surely respectable enough in sporting terms to justify the treatment it receives in these pages. Witness the club's claiming respective and successive intercontinental triumphs in the 2013 and 2014 editions of the Copa Libertadores and Recopa Sudamericana. At the same time, Atlético historically has failed to contend for league honors with the same consistency as bigger city sides, such as Flamengo, São Paulo FC, Corinthians, Santos, and Palmeiras—all of which brings us back to the COVID-wracked season of 2020. Originally scheduled for May 3 to December 6 on the calendar, this same installment of the Brasileirão was modified because of COVID-19 to run from August 8, 2020, to February 25, 2021. If Atlético did not prevail during this fateful season, which is now remembered as much for its endless complications regarding scheduling dilemmas and the maintenance of COVID protocols as it is for any joie de vivre that games might have produced on matchdays, CAM did give the competition's more fashionable sides a real run for their money.[16]

Insofar as *playing* entails more than winning and losing, the number of titles that Atlético Mineiro has secured over the last half century does little to help us comprehend what kicking a ball across a well-tended field for ninety minutes (plus stoppage time) could possibly mean in the context of COVID-19. *That Futebol Feeling* addresses this seeming contradiction without wholly resolving it. This is not to say that, as students of the game, we can just shift the burden of interpreting play to the players themselves; it is to suggest instead that even a partial rumination on the game of football such as this study comprises can only benefit from allowing the athletes who put their bodies on the proverbial line to speak to the motives and mind-sets that animate their willing participation in sport. Atlético, it should be noted, counted just under thirty first-team players during the memorable 2020 campaign; as with most teams, an ascertainable "starting eleven" (to use the popular footballing parlance) took shape over the course of the standard thirty-eight games.[17] My focus does not include all the members of this first-choice squad of regulars who braved the initial wave of COVID; professional football rosters mutate and change almost as fast as the most variable of viruses. But a few of the members of the 2020 side did continue with Atlético Mineiro long enough to warrant inclusion in what follows. They are survivors of a different kind: Not only did they perform well enough on the pitch to secure themselves a place on that COVID test-case of a team; they outlasted their then manager, the Argentine Jorge Sampaoli, who left Atlético in February 2021 after being offered the top job at the classy French side Olympique de Marseille.[18] In the open letter that Sampaoli addressed to Atlético's fan base upon his exit, he alludes to the worst of what Brazilians had been through amid a time of much suffering, but he also insists, in his own words, that although "2020 was a very tough year for humanity," he, his players, and staff had resolved "to build a team that . . . would make us forget about sadness for a moment." Sampaoli concludes, "We didn't just set out to win: we tried to be happy."[19] It may well be the case that "happiness" comes more readily to those who can afford a certain degree of complacency than it does to the rest of us. Sampaoli's players, after all, had already earned a special distinction in their sport, along with the saturation of media attention that comes with it, despite the fact that none of them was on a par (few players are) with Brazil's most iconic footballer, the Três Corações, Minas Gerais, native Pelé.[20] Nor were all the members of Sampaoli's side necessarily mineiros; some of them weren't even Brazilians. By listening to the *unreasonable* explanations of these Atlético professionals as they speak to their personal investments in play, however, we can begin to confirm an important sporting principle that appears to apply even under the worst of pandemic conditions. In short, these athletes might have traveled different paths to reach the top-flight of Brazilian football, but they all carry with them a proclivity for play that is, as a quotient of human desire, hard to quantify.[21] There are pluses and *Minases* to any method of reckoning with such abstractions, yet anyone with a propensity to wager would do well to take the "over" on emotion being a precipitating and sustaining condition of play for most *jogadores de futebol*.

If this characterization of Brazil's sporting culture sounds uplift-
ing, it is so only to the extent that it recognizes that these players
were not untouched by the very real hardships and uncertainties
the people of their country have experienced before and during
COVID times. Brazilians have long been beset by any number of
infectious diseases, whether borne by man or mosquito. There is
even a precedent for these diseases having had an adverse impact
on football, as when host city Rio de Janeiro was compelled to
postpone the South American Championship of Nations, or *Sul
Americano*, from 1918 to 1919 due to the worldwide influenza
epidemic that coincided with the closing stages of the First World
War.[22] In addition, systemic racism is as endemic to Brazil as it is
the United States. Poverty and crime are similarly widespread there,
and environmental depredation is ongoing, as it is everywhere on
Earth. Their obvious privileges notwithstanding, Atlético's players
have pursued their sport amid conditions that well might make
a mockery (if one were predisposed to laugh) of Brazil's national
motto, "*Ordem e Progresso*," a cognate phrase that translates as
"Order and Progress." Yet precisely because of these seeming para-
doxes, and irrespective of the growing justification we might have
for suspending all games, the *atleticanos* whose lives are chronicled
here embody a persevering spirit to *play* that warrants further scrutiny. Such is the purpose of this book.

Regardless of whatever else can be said about the football spirit,
I should emphasize that it amounts to more than a mere habit, a
learned behavior engrained in players after a lifetime of physical
conditioning and supervised training.[23] This spirit also transcends
the basic economic need for self-survival or, for some professionals,
the aspiration to obtain the comparative wealth that is the necessary corollary of a footballer's wages at the highest levels of the
sport. Of course, anyone who has watched football (from the side-
lines, the stands, or more likely while seated in front of a television,
handheld phone, tablet, or laptop) must concede that the spectacle
of the game can sometimes make for a rather uninspiring display.
There is a fine line, for example, in football between competitive
effort and licensed violence, as evidenced by the all-too-frequent in-
jury-inducing tackles that prompt commentators to remind us that

we are watching a "contact sport." It's also hard to deny the merchantable aspects of a sport whose lifeblood depends on the regular infusion of capital by a virtual cartel of club owners and corporate sponsors.[24] Even Brazil's prohibition against football clubs being run as for-profit enterprises has done little to stem the tide of football's monetization. The symbolic weight the game has carried in Brazilian society from the 1930s forward, moreover, as an index of the relative inclusiveness of the country's so-called tropical modernity has likewise made futebol (to use the proper Portuguese term) anything but a neutral venue for consumerist diversion or the abiding mission to harness discipline to art.[25] Football, in other words, may not be immune to the problems we find on and off the pitch, and it is surely distilled from more than the sources and expressions of our better natures. But the game retains an elusive quality, for players and spectators alike, that moves us even at those moments when we would otherwise remain unmoved. If this sporting life has a logic, it is a ludic one that reminds us that playfulness for its own sake can sometimes be its own reward.

To that end, Brazilians take pride in playing the game with a freedom and joy, or *alegria*, that some observers would liken to a national birthright. But to suggest that this quality of play is indicative of a distinctive *brasiliadade*, or essentialized "Brazilianness," that distinguishes native footballers from the Europeans who are said to have founded the sport upon rationalized principles of instrumental endeavor is to subscribe to the racialized understanding of the game that Brazilians themselves have struggled with over the last century.[26] The argument of this book is not that Brazilian footballers—and by implication, the many Afro-Brazilian common folk, or *povo*, who populate their ranks—are innately "playful," unreasoning, or childlike in their reputed primitiveness, at least not any more so than men and women raised in colder climes. Instead, *That Futebol Feeling* interrogates what the playing of the game means to the players of one nation, in one place, at a time when the reasons not to play are innumerable. The place that centers this study, to repeat, is the Brazilian state of Minas Gerais ("general mines," in English), home of the Série A club side Atlético Mineiro. As for the impetus to play, that varies from player to player as we survey the current and former members of Atlético who continued to suit up amid the fallout from COVID-19. What I can say at the outset is that a player's will to play should not be mistaken for a racial trait, an ethnic heritage, or a national signifier, any more than a footballer who manifests a modicum of playfulness on the pitch should suffer the indignity of warranting our consideration only to the degree that he first achieves the subject matter status of an "ontology," ideology, or socially endowed symbol.[27]

To be sure, the urge to play the game for its own sake could be said to share the same reflexive "goal" of all ideologies, which is to create and sustain the conditions under which any given ideology exists.[28] In staking its claim to a more subjective side of sport, however, above and beyond football's status as an emotionally charged marker for the far-reaching meanings of globalization,[29] *That Futebol Feeling* advances a series of implicit propositions that I hope will expand the bases on which football can be construed as fit for the consideration of nonparticipants in the game, not because of but despite its unquestioned political associations. Methodologically, this book posits that play can retain a humanist interest for students of culture without having to be subordinated to an analysis of the social dynamics of power. Intellectually, it contends that the impulse to examine the root feelings that inform sport need not be dismissed as innocent or naïve, even when this impulse relegates political consciousness as a topic to a position of secondary importance.[30] As the German cultural theorist Hans Ulrich Gumbrecht explains, there is a physical, material, and aesthetic pleasure to all variety of athletic performances that derives from the "distance" that separates sport from "the interests and strategies that make up our everyday world." The "joy" that we experience when we indulge this pleasure is enough of a philosophical justification to appreciate football as a way of being in the world that need not qualify as escapist.[31] And, finally, *That Futebol Feeling* serves as a timely reminder that we don't have to be world-class athletes to think of ourselves as *players*. We are all in the game simply by virtue of being here, by being alive in the web of relations and emotions that sport ideally forges, not least in times of crisis. I am, therefore, working with as capacious an understanding of *player* as is possible with this project, the better to demonstrate the common bonds that play facilitates within and around the world of sport. Professional athletes, supporters, and administrators, as well as coaches, writers, artists, and corporate executives, can all qualify as "players" in my estimation. And in this book, they do.

A Cock and Bull Story

Atlético Mineiro's totemic animal mascot bears the honorific *Galo*, Portuguese for "the Rooster" or "the Cock." Sporting the club's colors of black and white, Galo is the symbolic embodiment of CAM; he represents Atlético's fan base in the aggregate, which is also known as *A Massa*, meaning "the mass" (Figure 1.1). More than that, and as one immoderate Atlético supporter boasts on the personal website he maintains on behalf of his team, Galo is "the name that most radically and truly expresses, for so many millions of Brazilians," a "passion" that resides in the very "soul of the fans." Our same enthusiast is quick to dismiss the powers of competitors' mascots while asserting the Cock's status atop the hierarchy of the domestic game. For this Atlético stalwart, the Vulture (Flamengo), the Pig (Palmeiras), the Fish (Santos), the Fox (Cruzeiro), and the Lion (Inter de Limeira, which currently plays in the top tier of the São Paulo state football league) are all inferior creatures. Yet what is most revealing in this taxonomy is that it signals its creator's willingness to subsume his identity in the collective affective attachment to the Clube that is synonymous with his Cause. No matter the score line at the sound of any full-time whistle, Galo knows what it knows because it feels what it feels. Galo is the consummate romantic in this respect. For what Galo feels, tautologically speaking, is that feeling is everything in football, that victory and defeat amount to the same thing—or almost the same thing—when, again in the words of Galo's self-anointed spokesman, "a goal, a championship, a hug or a kiss" are all equivalent indicators of what it means to carry the Rooster's emotions upon the signature vertical black-and-white stripes of the team's sleeves.[32]

We can only speculate as to how these feelings have helped Atlético negotiate COVID-19. Reports coming out of Belo Horizonte

Figure 1.1 Clube Atlético Mineiro's
Galo, the "Rooster" icon and
nickname that is the Brasileirão
side's universal signifier. (*Courtesy
Clube Atlético Mineiro.*)

on November 17, 2020, revealed that no fewer than nine members
of the club had tested positive for the coronavirus: the bald-pated,
tattoo-armed, sixty-year-old coach Sampaoli; his immediate assis-
tants; several fitness coaches; the goalkeeping coach; one player;
and the organization's communications director. Composed by the
Minas Gerais native Vicente Mota in 1969, the opening lines of
Atlético's anthem proclaim CAM's resilience and readiness to rise
to any challenge. "We are from Clube Atlético Mineiro," the lyric
begins, "We play with a lot of *raça* and *amor*, / We vibrate with joy
in victories."[33] In COVID, of course, Atlético had met an altogether
different variety of opponent, meaning that the team would *mais
ou menos* need to confront the virus with all the "raça and amor"
(the former Portuguese word connoting an inner strength and grit,
the latter denoting love) it celebrates in song. As it turned out, all
of those afflicted among this first wave of positive cases at the
club proved to be either asymptomatic or showed only mild symptoms. Still, even a Brazilian government led by the country's then-
president, the controversial Jair Bolsonaro, who asserted in late
December that the coronavirus vaccines being developed outside
his country could turn their recipients into "crocodiles," treated

COVID-19 with serious enough consideration to allow the British-based multinational pharmaceutical conglomerate AstraZeneca to conduct trials for its own patented vaccine in Brazil.[34] These trials were mismanaged and eventually declared inconclusive by their sponsors. They additionally, and admittedly, belong to a considerable body of evidence surrounding the full term of Bolsonaro's ill-fated administration that places great pressure upon my determination to remain agnostic on the question of politics in my treatment of play. In any case, given that Brasileirão matches continued to be played behind closed doors at the start of the new year, it stands to reason that league officials, if not everyone inside the national government, perceived the threat COVID-19 posed to the public health of even the mighty Galo. Atlético, meanwhile, began 2021 tied for first place in the league table, with a game in hand over São Paulo FC one week into January.

As a pernicious virus, COVID-19 is clearly no fable; the myth of the Rooster, by contrast, resists objective analysis. Such interpretive resistance is to be expected from any model of wishful thinking that pretends to have discovered a way to mold some subset of disparate selves into a voluntary society of believers. Most citizens of the United States, for instance, would attest that the sleight-of-hand solidarity behind the concept *e pluribus unum* (out of many, one) remains as illusory a civic ideal as the trick that Galo is imagined to perform by amalgamating Atlético's masses into a single cohesive entity, which latter feat of partisan football magic has been captured so viscerally in director Cris Azzi's award-winning 2014 documentary of loyal atleticanos, *O dia do Galo*.[35] Surely something instructive lies in these examples of "team" cohesion for Brazilians who have thought about their country's own struggles over the course of the twentieth century to consolidate as a modern nation-state. More to the point of this project, Galo's feelings for football are not necessarily the same as those of Atlético's players, despite the tacit assumption of most fans that their consensual absorption by the club would have a coalescing effect for CAM. In the end, the supporters have their feelings; the players have theirs. Both sets of feelings are of concern in this study, even if the athletes' respective perspectives on the game they play continue to account for a relatively underexamined aspect of an otherwise pervasive contemporary conversation on sport.[36]

Advances in data analytics have no doubt provided us with fresh talking points about the various competitions in which professional athletes engage, presumably on our behalf. What we risk sacrificing by relying too heavily upon numbers for telling our stories of sport is any meaningful discussion of the emotions that footballers, specifically, bring to their game. Players predictably evince ambivalence about the performance-oriented metrics that now determine everything from matchday tactics to squad selection. Some of them embrace big data; others have their misgivings; many more waver in their opinions about this and much else besides. *That Futebol Feeling* acknowledges the value of having these updated conversations but chooses to initiate an alternative one instead. Whatever else a professional football player might be, he is widely regarded, as the Uruguayan writer Eduardo Galeano observes, as "the . . . athlete who escaped the factory or the office and gets paid to have fun."[37] This book duly sets out to assess the quantity and the quality of footballers' fun, as measured by the passion for playing that Atlético's regulars may or may not carry with them to and from the "job" that pays their bills, bruises their bodies, and subjects them to the relentless attention of a not-always-admiring public. Without intending to underwrite the shaping of any additional creation myths, *That Futebol Feeling* accordingly heeds the emotional lives of players whose actions on the pitch typically represent the extent of what we "know" about them, the digital intimacies afforded by twenty-four-hour news cycles, club websites, TV channels, and social networks notwithstanding.

Further complicating the telling of this present narrative about football and feeling are the mixed emotions of the players mentioned earlier. In the masterful history of Clube Atlético Mineiro that he composed "from the stands," Brazilian author (and Atlético supporter) Ricardo Galuppo takes to heart the lyrical (il)logic of Galo's belief system, premised as it is on equal parts raça and amor. Galuppo finds nothing contradictory about Galo's twin preparedness to love and to fight, to compete and to play. "Since its foundation," he explains, CAM "has been a defender of good causes" without allowing its convictions to harden into prejudices, and without permitting its most forcefully felt feelings to inhibit the greater good that is fair play. "Football is not war—it is peace and joy," Galuppo writes, with the assurance of the initiate that his "faith" provides for what he describes as "a possibility of *alegria* on earth."[38] Echoing the sentiments (before COVID-19) of a member of the CAM supporters' group Torcida Organizada Dragões da F.A.O., however, Galuppo admits that the condition of A Massa is unconditional—that is, he likens raça and amor to a "black and white microbe that gets into people's blood and doesn't come out at all."[39] In other words, Galuppo operates on the emotional assumption that his love for his club is something that exists under the skin. Or, to borrow the name of the subscription-based CAM benefits card "Galo Na Veia," a twenty-first-century supporter of Atlético only begins to qualify as such once the passion that he or she feels for his or her side has gotten *into the veins*, not unlike a virus.[40] It would be difficult to diagnose an affliction that doubles as an affection. Not only that, and to return to the problem of distinguishing between the feelings of fans and the feelings of footballers, we have no reliable basis of even knowing with any certainty whether players want to be infected by the club of their heart, or *clube do coração*.[41]

The Atlético players whom Galuppo portrays in his history betray enough of the symptoms of sentiment to suggest that they are indeed moved by emotions, but their feelings about football don't necessarily reduce to raça and amor. There is, to begin, the feeling of socially conscious righteousness that players and supporters alike have nurtured from the club's beginning. Founded in 1908 by a group of twenty-two upper-class secondary school students, civil servants, and working professionals in Belo Horizonte, Athletico Mineiro Foot-Ball Club, as CAM was then known, began as an amateur institution (as did all football clubs in those days) with a difference: Rather than being tied to any particular social group or ethnic enclave, the modest young men who established themselves as a "people's club" decided early on that they would not discriminate according to race, class, religion, or nationality. All were welcome at Athletico, and consequently the team attracted the largest

Figure 1.2 Clube Atlético Mineiro in the early days, from 1914. (*Courtesy Clube Atlético Mineiro.*)

fan base in the surrounding city and state. Our founding *mineiros* could also play. Against the backdrop of the tree-lined streets and unpaved roads of their native Belo Horizonte, they won the inaugural installment of the Campeonato Mineiro in 1915 before repeating as champions in 1925 (Figure 1.2). As this labor was unpaid, the players who helped secure these titles sweated for fun during the Sunday afternoon kickabouts that marked, in retrospect, a transitional period for the sport in Brazil. For when Atlético Mineiro reconstituted itself as a professional sports organization in 1933, the club's cherished principle of equal access thereafter had to coexist with its not entirely welcome practice of pay for play. Other clubs in the city raised strenuous objections as Atlético ironically, if temporarily, ceded the populist moral high ground to its neighbors.[42]

CAM has since suffered periodically from the new era of high finance in football that this episode foretold. It was already one of the most heavily indebted clubs in the Brazilian league by the 1950s. The debts kept mounting in the halcyon days of the 1970s, despite the fanfare with which the decade started. CAM's finances continued to deteriorate in the 1990s, only for the team to be forced to join with other top sides in the Brasileirão in 2015 to enter an agreement with the federal government (Atlético's largest creditor) to refinance its tax debts under the legislative Program for Modernization of Management and Fiscal Responsibility of Brazilian Football, or Profut.[43] Brazil's president at the time, Dilma Rousseff, might have made no secret of being an Atlético supporter, but she was not about to allow the financial mismanagement of her country's highest-profile sports organizations, CAM included, to further burden the nation as it slipped into an economic recession.[44] However well-intentioned these reforms were, Atlético has persisted alongside other clubs in permitting outlays on players' salaries that far exceed its revenue, such that it had accrued outstanding loans in the amount of a reputed R\$1.3 billion (roughly US\$257 million) as of 2021.[45] None of this debt would have overly concerned Atlético's players, provided they continued to be paid at a moment when COVID-19 had straitened the club's finances even more than before.[46] Such has been the legacy of financial difficulty at Clube Atlético Mineiro that one must nonetheless wonder how motivated these same players are to perform for an employer that, if not on the brink of insolvency, has occasionally flirted with the humiliating prospect of relegation to the second tier of Brazilian football.[47] If nothing else, the feelings that must still flow for today's players from CAM's original egalitarian pretensions could only be experienced by them equivocally.

As these questionable financial dealings should demonstrate, not all the feelings associated with CAM are pure. In fact, some of the emotions manifested by the club's players on the field of play are purely "ugly," to apply to football Sianne Ngai's formulation for those "negative" feelings within our culture (envy, anxiety, and irritation, among others) that we struggle to reconcile with our more exalted sense of ourselves.[48] If raça and amor represent Galo at his aspirational best, then he draws on a substratum of feelings to play a game that, like the world it portends, is anything but Atlético black and white. Thus, maybe it was rage and not just an excess of raça that induced Kafunga, the goalkeeper who represented CAM from 1935 to 1955, to impose himself physically on his teammates during training sessions, to the point that the team's strikers, who otherwise lined up on the same side of the field as him on matchdays, knew better than to ever try to put the ball past their own shot stopper.[49] Then there is Reinaldo, the club's all-time leading goalscorer and consensus best player, who netted 255 times for Atlético—at an average rate of 1.55 goals per match in the 1977 season, still the highest figure in league history—over the course of his 475 appearances for CAM between 1973 and 1985. A Massa loved *o Rei*, as they punningly named him. Opposing players brutalized "the King," bringing a halt to his jinking runs with fouls that were so insistent, they left Reinaldo in need of no fewer than nine surgeries (many of them on his much-harried knees) by the time he was twenty-one.[50] If alegria has a dark side in the Brazilian game, then Reinaldo experienced it more than most. But, aside from his political sentiments—"the King" openly opposed the military dictatorship that seized control of the country in 1964 and so took to celebrating his goals with a raised fist of defiance toward the regime—a player whom the national opposition newspaper *Movimento* metonymically described as *"Bom de bola, bom de cuca"* (Good on the ball, right in the head) felt a greater weight of responsibility to his club than he did resentment against competitors. It is true that the seriousness with which Reinaldo took to his trade did nothing to dampen his playfulness on the pitch. "I don't worry about the opponent, only the ball," he has said. But from the start of his playing days at CAM, *o Rei* recognized that his performances for Atlético were ultimately undertaken in the service of something, or someone, larger than himself.[51] Marcelo Oliveira, another superlative striker for the *alvinegro*, or "white-and-black," similarly recalled losing the Brasileirão title to São Paulo FC (on penalties) on the final day of the 1977 season as "the saddest day of my life."[52] His emotions no doubt hurt him more because he knew that Atlético had succumbed—unfairly, Galo maintains to this day—to an establishment side that A Massa suspects benefitted from a vague favoritism (whether divine or human, it would be hard to say) that was denied to the likes of the humble side from Belo Horizonte. There is little joy to be found in such feelings.

Then again, Galo has never enjoyed unqualified happiness. Galuppo expresses this sentiment best when he writes, with what could be a credo for the club he loves, "As an *atleticano*, I have lived deep sadness."[53] And yet it would be hard to argue that the author hasn't simply given utterance to emotions here that most fans of football know by heart. They, too, have probably been conditioned enough by feelings of defeat to agree that dejection and disappointment are the tandem side of desire when it takes the form of sport. Unlike Galo, not every footballer takes pride in a feeling, if not of inferiority, than of having assumed a mantle of hard luck that may be more apparent than real, considering CAM's history of success and its membership since 1987 in the *Clube dos Treze*, or what is officially known as the "Union of Great Brazilian Football Clubs."[54] For every television broadcaster like Luiz Eduardo Schechtel—*Dudu Galo Doido* (Crazy Rooster), as A Massa calls him—shedding tears of distress for CAM before the cameras of the much-watched Minas Gerais program *Alterosa esportes* during matches at the start of this century, there may well be a player who eases his way through contests harboring the "negative" emotion of boredom that is far more prevalent in sports than we would expect.[55] As a boy, Galuppo writes, Dudu "understood, emotionally, the meaning of being *atleticano*."[56] The question is whether Atlético's players share this same understanding—or, perhaps the more pertinent thing to ask is why they would want to, when the sadness that is implied by Galo's presumption of perpetual suffering might be offset by the alegria that football, in happier times, would allow them to enjoy.

A Personal Word about This Book

COVID-19 remains with us as I write these lines, meaning that it may be too soon to flatter ourselves into the belief that we have somehow outlived the worst of its attendant disturbances. Meanwhile, the living and breathing among us are returning to some semblance of our former selves now that we're (I hope) vaccinated, boosted, and convinced of our own relative safety. It is a sign of our collective resilience, hubris, or both that we can begin again to ask for a little joy from life, a little alegria, now that we have demonstrated to our own satisfaction that there is a future that includes us. Whatever else we have in common, we share a pandemic that no longer allows us to take that future for granted.

And so here I am, writing these lines from Belo Horizonte, Brazil, while making progress on a book about play as it pertains to my adopted club, Atlético Mineiro. As a professor of nineteenth-century American literature at the University of Rhode Island, in the United States, I can identify with the words of one of my countrymen, the poet Walt Whitman, when he announces himself as being "both in and out of the game, and watching and wondering at it."[57] That is, I am a lifelong fan of football, and I like to believe that I am as capable as anyone of responding to it with the emotions it deserves. I'm in the game as much as I can be, not being a "player" in the same way that CAM squad members, such as the midfielder Allan or the incomparably named forward "Hulk" (Givanildo Vieira de Sousa), are. A cultural critic to boot, I nevertheless maintain by principle and in practice a critical distance from my subject matter. It would be difficult in the extreme, if not impossible, to play the game the way that Atlético's rock-solid Paraguayan defender Júnior Alonso does and still be able to think about raça, say, or maybe amor, without prejudice. With Whitman, then, I watch and wonder at football even though I am not quite involved in the game in any immediate sense and my critical faculties remain mostly intact.

Whether I'm actually "working" while I think and write about culture—in this case, the culture of play that exists in sport—is another matter. In fact, I have struggled with this question throughout my academic career. The study of literature has always been fun for me, and perhaps this enjoyment was why I was drawn to literary study in the first place. Indeed, perhaps this is how I know it to be my calling. I should stress, however, that I take a decidedly historicist approach to my discipline in my teaching and my research; thus, the postmodern interest in the free "play" of endless signifiers is not what attracts me to critical literary studies, any more than I believe in art for art's sake. What I do believe, and what I could not take more seriously, is that the mandate of cultural studies to "read" culture in its manifold forms—whether that form be the game of football, a film, or a novel—holds the potential to reveal to us the underlying causes and effects of how we organize our everyday lives. From this perspective, football or some other form of "play" need not be seen as occupying a separate sphere of *lazer*, or leisure; it might instead be interpreted as a constituent part of what we are, who we are, and why we are the way we are. To meditate on such matters in no way feels like play to me, and if it is play, then it is a game that I have chosen to play with purpose.

It is still not clear to me whether I chose Galo or Galo chose me. What I did precipitate was a four months' residence in Belo Horizonte between May and September 2022. To clarify, it was not fate that brought me to Atlético Mineiro; it was a position as Fulbright Distinguished Chair in Studies of the United States at the Universidade Federal de Minas Gerais (UFMG), where I *worked* while teaching an undergraduate course on the American short story and a graduate seminar (in the university's Political Science Department, no less) in American politics and literature. The place and the program of my stay were of my own choosing, then, but this is not to say that I controlled the timing of my travels. To disclose more of myself than I would like, I submitted my application for the award that I was eventually granted back in July 2019. Divorced in 2014 and having just seen a subsequent five-year relationship come to a painful close, I was feeling the need for some sort of transformative change, apparently one underwritten by the U.S. State Department. My academic research at the time just so happened to be focused on the nineteenth-century use of Benjamin Franklin's *Poor Richard's Almanack* as an elementary textbook in the primary schools of Minas Gerais, and the change (of scenery, sensibility, and scholarship) that I was looking for at that juncture presented itself to me with such starkness that I could not ignore it. To trivialize things, I could say that having lost at love, I won a Fulbright, even though I am reticent to reduce my life to a "game" in this way. If my motives weren't any purer than the feelings of the footballers whom I have already mentioned, then I never doubted the sincerity of my having long wanted to be a Fulbright fellow at some point in my career. Nor would I even begin to describe my feelings for Galo as merely compensatory. Let me be frank about this: The potential opportunity that I had to get closer to the club I'd come to love was an unexpected boon, to be sure. But, with a legitimate need to visit the Arquivo Público Mineiro to learn more about *Bom homem Ricardo*, as Brazilians have come to call the universally recognized text from Ben Franklin that carries his eponymous persona's name, and with a genuine desire to teach at UFMG, I could feel Belo Horizonte beckon. Then, COVID struck, and the welcome news that I'd heard from the Fulbright Commission in April 2020 of the success of my application was suddenly little more than provisional. Confined at home for the most part like many Americans, I kept inside and bided my time for *Brasil*, hoping, if not expecting, that my scheduled trip could be deferred. It was, and not once but twice, to the southern hemispheric winter of 2022. The difficulties that I experienced in an interim period of waiting and wishing were offset by my general good health in these years. The same could not be said for my mother, who nearly died from COVID-19 in El Paso, Texas, during the pestilential summer of 2020. To repeat, and being careful of how I choose my words, life is no game.

My mother has improved markedly since the time of her ten-day confinement in an American hospital's intensive care unit in the U.S. desert southwest, fighting for enough oxygen to survive, and yet the mood of my early weeks in Belo Horizonte was dampened somewhat by a kind of survivor's remorse. People were and are still dying from COVID-19, while American professors on leave in South America work at playing as scholars of sport. I could hardly blame my mood on the weather. Fall and winter in Belo Horizonte are mostly sunny, dry, and mild. And even though my walks around this hilly city ("Belo Hills," the locals call it) were opening up my mind, and heart, to a place I'd wanted to see firsthand, I always seemed to be heading *uphill* whenever I headed outside for an amble around the neighborhood where I lived, Barro Preto. The latter *bairro* is, of course, the historic home of CAM's inner-city foe Cruzeiro, so perhaps the reservations I carried with me stemmed from my feeling like a Cock on the wrong side of the block whenever I skulked by the nearby empty service garage–like facility that doubles as the mildly menacing hangout for the Fox's "Blue Mafia" supporters' group on Rua dos Timbiras.[58] In fairness, Atlético Mineiro's territorial reach in the city and state is as vast as the club's fans are legion in these parts. Neither infected with

COVID-19 nor generally foul of disposition, I must have been troubled, I surmise, after arriving in the city where I would be living by something seated deep in my feelings about feelings. These feelings are, I have intimated, a recurring source of worry for me as I work at what most people would consider a post-adolescent form of play. The fact that I have so far written this much about the emotional components of play suggests that I have not been deterred in my work. And, not to overdramatize the import of how an eccentric American should spend his vital time on Earth, suffice it to say that I am untroubled enough by the contradictions of my working life to own up to my long-standing fixation with football. What's more, I remain convinced of the worth of doing the work that my passion entails—hence the reflexive nature of my project, which asks that we examine the very meanings of our passions.

Having attended to these preliminaries, I can address how this book materialized and how the rest of it unfolds. The pandemic's continuation notwithstanding, 2022 turned out to be an auspicious year for me and CAM. In December 2021, Atlético Mineiro secured its first Brasileirão title in fifty years. They began the new year as reigning champions of a league in which Atlético had grown accustomed to finishing second or third best. That same year, I turned fifty, awakened (halfway?) through my course of life like the narrator from the medieval Italian poet Dante Alighieri's fourteenth-century epic verse the *Divine Comedy*. I was ready to seek grace and Galo in warmer climes. In Dante's telling, the journey for renewal begins in hell; mine started closer to heaven, in Belo Horizonte—or, rather, it started on the campus of UFMG, located in the city's northern Pampulha neighborhood. I had been told before my arrival in Brazil that Belo Horizonte was big enough that it was impossible to know everyone, but, at approximately 2.7 million people, it was small enough that I was liable to know someone who knew someone, who knew someone. And so it proved. A colleague of mine in UFMG's Ciencia Política department, Ricardo Fabrino Mendonça, fortuitously turned out to be an acquaintance of a member of Clube Atlético Mineiro's board, the administrative headquarters for which sit in the city's central Lourdes district, about a fifteen-minute stroll from my home. Another colleague in the university's Office of International Relations, Luciana Fiuza, is Galo through and through; she is also, almost improbably, a sometime next-door neighbor in Belo Horizonte's southern region of *o Rei*, CAM's tremendous goal-getter Reinaldo, and has a COVID-convalescent journalist sister whose boss is close friends with a footballer whom many rate as one of the nation's all-time greats. I interpreted these coincidences for what they were—coincidences—even as I gratefully accepted them as an entrée into CAM's inner circle, where the players who are what Elcio Loureiro Cornelsen calls the "protagonists" of Brazilian football play.[59]

More than coincidence made this book possible; my work has benefited from the cooperation of many members from the Galo community. CAM's administrators opened their doors to me to discuss the Clube. Two more colleagues at UFMG from the school's program in Letras—Elcio Loureiro Cornelsen and Marcelino Rodrigues da Silva, both members of the working group FuLiA, Nucleus of Studies on Football, Language, and Arts—shared their research on the Brazilian game while providing encouragement and welcome counsel on my own. Then, there are the players. Without a doubt, they had more pressing matters to attend to than answering questions philosophical ("How would you describe alegria to someone who has never played the game?") and nonsensical ("What are your earliest football memories?") posed to them by a bespectacled, COVID-masked stranger who is slight of build and scarce of hair, and whose pidgin spoken Portuguese owes nothing to the superior instruction he received while enrolled in Analia Tebaldi's online course in POR 101 at the University of Massachusetts Dartmouth in the spring semester of 2022. And yet the players graciously gave their time and attention to me to think and talk about play as a facet of their work. These conversations did not take place at the stately Estadio Mineirão, still, at that time, the flagship stadium for Clube Atlético Mineiro before the team's move in April 2023 to the new forty-six-thousand-seat Arena MRV. Nor did we speak at CAM's state-of-the-art training facility, Cidade do Galo (Rooster City), located in the Vespasiano municipality, some twenty-seven kilometers to the north of Belo Horizonte. COVID-19 restrictions had rendered the latter site off-limits to all nonessential personnel. Wherever we met, online or in person across the city, our encounters must have felt interminable to the players. They could not have lasted long enough for me.

The results of these conversations are the substance of what you are now reading. Thinking (and feeling) like a player, I have named this introductory chapter "Pre-match," my reason being that it approximates those moments before a game when our attention is afforded a degree of time and space for reflection that is not available to us once a contest begins in earnest. In truth, not the least of the artistic liberties *That Futebol Feeling* takes is to pause this interval for taking stock indefinitely, so that we come to occupy a temporal ever-present in which clocks never run down and players, especially, retain a kind of ambidextrous capacity for giving their runs, jumps, kicks, crosses, and feints a second (or even a first) thought. To this extent "*Raça*," the next chapter in this study, takes a prolonged look at what may be CAM's distinguishing emotional feature, the never-say-die attitude that the club likes to say that it maintains in all contests and contexts. For an author, the danger in accepting without question this aspect of Galo's interested self-posturing is that he or she begins to see the club through the eyes of the supporter—which, in this case, he is. Thus, I let the players do much of the talking in this portion of the book, hoping that they can articulate for themselves what it *feels* like to play for a side, Atlético Mineiro—a team many of them didn't even grow up supporting—that stakes its identity on fielding a squad that gives maximum effort and commitment, if not always to winning, then certainly to avoiding defeat. Depending on one's perspective, the emotional temper that we might conclude exists within so intense a sporting environment would probably have little to offer to the faint of heart, nor would it necessarily qualify as the most hospitable place to play, as observers tend to agree that play as a form of behavior usually lacks an obvious goal.[60] What I try to elicit from CAM's players, then, in my conversational exchanges with them is an awareness of the seeming conundrums in which their current or former sporting situations with Atlético placed them. One, they were playing for pay. Two, they played for a club for which they might not possess a particular passion. Three, the ethos of the side for whom they suited up could be felt as anathema to the very spirit of play. And four, of course, they were still playing against a pandemic that just wouldn't quit.

Invariably following *"Raça"* is the chapter I've titled *"Amor,"* love being the emotional counterpoint to a steely determination that, if considered in isolation, might otherwise make Galo estimable but, I confess, unlovable. "Amor" cuts to the heart of what play promised when we were little: fun, frolic, the thrill of going nowhere in particular and enjoying every (unaccounted for) minute of it. By no means would I have us reconceive of a group of professional footballers as children. Rather, I want to highlight how people whom we categorically identify as "players" conceive of themselves in the minutes when they are on the pitch or openly emoting for the Clube, and whether they are playing, preparing to play, or caring about the game they adore. COVID-19 without question has complicated such love as players are able to express for a pastime that now constitutes a paycheck. Amor, furthermore, and as we have already seen, must be considered in relation to the raça to which Galo trusts it is inseparably wed. Even with all these potential hindrances, however, Atlético's players still play the game of futebol with a skill and abandon suggesting that they feel more than an obligation to do so. The reason for this book's being is to ask why, to question what it is that brings the players of one team, at one time, to attach feeling to the meaning of sport.

The "post-match" chapter that closes this study represents another of my willful postponements, which I make to allow us to linger once more to think about where the game of football can carry us in our emotional negotiations of life. As should be clear by now, my own life has played out in different places under sometimes difficult circumstances, as is the norm for those of us who have opened ourselves up emotionally to the sport that we all love. It would be fair to say, in my own case, that I've experienced my share of sorrows along the way, as well as a surprising number of joys, more even than I can remember. *That Futebol Feeling* is a work of remembrance in this respect, as I want to ensure that I don't forget what and where football has allowed me to feel at times when my emotions might otherwise have gotten the better of me. Then again, the unifying argument that runs throughout this book is that the feelings that football inspires represent the best of me. Those who already share this feeling know what I mean. For those who don't, please allow me to explain.

2

Raça

Do you still remember my Theory of Human Editions?

—Machado de Assis, *Memorías póstumas de Brás Cubas*, 1880[1]

It seems only fitting that my research on life, death, work, and play should lead me to a fitness club. That's where I found myself at 8:00 A.M. on a Monday morning in late May 2022, in the middle-class neighborhood of Sion, in the southern precincts of Belo Horizonte. The gym itself, an *academia*, as the Brazilians call it, could not have been nicer, nor could the owner and operator of the establishment, Manoel Rezende de Mattos Cabral, have been a more gracious host. Guiding me past rows of well-intentioned patrons—all of them "working out"—into the mirror-lined sanctuary of his backroom office, the former footballer, who's still known as "Nelinho," engaged me in an hour-long conversation about the emotional component of the game he once played at the highest level. Capped twenty-one times by the Brazilian national team, or *Seleção* (the "Selects"), between the years 1974 and 1980, this veteran of two World Cups was, for a period in the late 1970s, considered by some to be the best right back on the planet. He still looked the part at the age of seventy-one. He furthermore spoke about *futebol* that day with the gentle authority of someone who had earned the right to do so. Having appeared in 401 matches for Atlético Mineiro's crosstown rivals Cruzeiro, and another 274 for Clube Atlético Mineiro (CAM), where he concluded his playing days in 1987, Nelinho knew a thing or two about *raça* (pronounced '*hasa*), among other sporting topics more and less esoteric.[2]

As for raça, "You either have it or you don't," Nelinho assured me.[3] Sure, he could recall players who liked to boast on the training pitch about having more cold-bloodedness than their peers, but Nelinho was having none of it. Raça remained for him something that a player draws on from his finite internal resources. It's a product of nature, not nurture, albeit a nature that was perhaps negotiable under certain circumstances. Nelinho regarded *raça e amor* as being mutually reinforcing, for instance, such that the player with "love" in his heart—for his team, for the game of futebol itself—will naturally have deep reserves of raça. Similarly, Nelinho conceded that any of the less technically gifted players who wanted to contend for a starting spot in the Atlético squad (the question of whether a Cruzeiro player could have raça was not one he cared to entertain) had to rely on raça more than others who were blessed with greater strength, speed, or touch.[4] I didn't have to ask whether Nelinho himself had exhibited raça as a player; his square jaw, sturdy shoulders, and overall hale appearance answered that tacit question. But I did walk out the door of his business that day wondering and worrying whether I now had any greater understanding of raça than I did before. Whatever impediments I was still dealing with in my ongoing initiation into *A Massa* were surely indicative of my own shortcomings, as "true" *atleticanos* did not need to have raça explained to them at the start of what was otherwise, for most people in Minas Gerais, just another work week. It was nevertheless hard not to feel that raça did need further deconstructing if it remained something that everyone among the Galo faithful knew about, regularly sang about, but perhaps seldom thought about, at least not in a manner that would allow them to assist a self-styled American football enthusiast to become any wiser on a subject that was chapter and verse to them. There was simply no understanding the feeling of *being* a player for CAM unless I could find a way to express an emotion that is, by widespread agreement, synonymous with the side I supported. The why and wherefore of raça, therefore, needed to be put into words, and that was a form of work I was able to undertake.

But, as Frederico Bolivar reminded me, "Football is very complicated."[5] Such has been Atlético's impression on "Bolivar," whom Brazilians remember as a member of the *Alterosa esporte* broadcast team from ten years ago, that he's joined the ranks of the *atleticano roxo*. These are the "purple" supporters who sympathize with the Clube so much that it hurts, their love being like a bruise that penetrates deep beneath the skin. More to the point, this *roxo* recognizes that raça can't be reduced to an easy formula for the convenience of writers, let alone foreign ones. Raça is messy, for one thing. Speaking from Lisbon, where he now works as a lawyer, journalist, and sports management consultant (including for CAM), Bolivar reported with pride that Atlético's regulars "play with their guts" and show "a readiness to die fighting."[6] Bolivar also wanted me to understand that the quantity and quality of raça vary from position to position. Individual players all need to attend to their specific duties on the pitch, and their raça will manifest according to the requirements of the roles they have been asked to fulfill. It's a compelling theory, but not one that relieves me of the need to rationalize an intestinal fortitude that was beginning to sound like a malady I might want to avoid. "Every team has its DNA," Bolivar continued, perhaps flattering me to think that I might someday understand the sequencing of CAM's genetic code. Yet as he went on to speak about the "synergy" between raça e amor, I sensed that our conversation was maybe leading me in circles.[7] As "complicated" as football is, my inquiries into raça were bringing me to the realization that not only did different observers subscribe to subtly (or not) variant versions of something that was supposedly inimitably Atlético; they were all too polite to relate the hard truth that I was going to have to feel raça for myself before I could begin to comprehend it.

In the meantime, there were additional factors to consider pertaining to this feeling. Brazilian anthropologist Roberto DaMatta attributes the popularity of futebol in his country to the unique position the sport occupies there in the minds of its many domestic fans. DaMatta contends that whereas North Americans tend to view all sports as a competition, an arena for the assertion of "physical control and the coordination of individuals to form a collectivity," Brazilians conceive of futebol in more individualistic terms, "as a *game* . . . an activity that requires tactics, strength, psychological and physical determination, [and] technical ability," but that also "depends on the uncontrollable forces of luck and destiny."[8] In other words, DaMatta views futebol in Brazil as a contest between "desire" and "destiny," between "biographies on the one side and collectivities governed by impersonal laws on the other" (106). This belief is not to suggest that footballers are resigned to a fate that the football gods decide on their behalf. Instead, DaMatta contends, the thinking (and feeling) in Brazil is that in football, as in politics, an ability to *play* combined with a mind for tactics and strategy are never a guarantee of victory; an element of luck is always involved, too, such that the outcomes of even the "easiest" contests can never be taken for granted (106, 110). Thus, precisely because football *is* political in Brazil—Brazilian men "discuss" (*discutir*) politics and futebol, DaMatta explains, while they merely "talk about" women and work—the sport operates as more than a metaphor even for people inside the country who would prefer not to preoccupy themselves with play. Futebol, rather, functions here as a forum for serious reflection on such perennial "national problems" as the question of how much hard work and hard luck, respectively, (pre)determine social mobility in a hierarchical society, which Brazil unquestionably remains. But, according to DaMatta, Brazilians don't just contemplate play; they *feel* it as well, such that they color their "alternating intellectual perception" of the game with the "lived experiences of emotions and sentiments" that endow their favorite sport with the high level of appeal that it maintains season after season (118). Indeed, it's always the season for feeling futebol in Brazil. There is hardly an interval on the calendar when the game is not being played somewhere.

For my part, I concede the importance of sport to Brazilian society while asking that we consider this mutually sustaining relationship from the opposite perspective. That is, I would have the game itself assume pride of place in any assessment of Brazilian life, so that "society" as such must carry the metaphorical burden of explaining what sport "means," rather than vice versa. I'm asking that we consider the possibility that the answer to the question of which came first, society or sport, may not be as obvious as we'd like to believe.

To return the conversation to CAM, recalibrating our interpretive expectations of sport might well entail regarding raça as the "reality" that obtains inside a social matrix where giving one's guts amounts to an outward sign of a personal (pre)disposition to carry play well past the normative boundaries of playfulness. Driving around Belo Horizonte, for instance, one can't help but notice all the street signs pointing traffic *out* of the city. These can be found among the canopy of trees and overhanging streetlamps that are tucked away even among the apartment towers of what seem to be the most contented residential neighborhoods. I spent years waiting to get into the city, so I was in no hurry to leave. But perhaps to the locals, who reside in a society that contrives to constantly remind them of the hinterland status of their state, the tangible allure of the wider world serves as a welcome reminder that they can exit when- and however they wish, that fate has not consigned them to a place they may experience as purgatory. Rio de Janeiro is this way, São Paulo that. The scenic colonial-era capital of Ouro Preto (Black Gold) lies straight ahead, while the closest beaches of nearby Vitória, in neighboring Espírito Santo state, can be reached by heading over there. For my part, I began to read these ubiquitous roadside markers as a corollary for the spirit of self-determination that CAM's players display whenever they take to the pitch—or perhaps I was simply observing the civilian equivalent of the modern Brazilian fairy tale. During the era of football's professionalization in Brazil between 1930 and 1950, the storyline would have had *mestiço* athletes of obvious mixed-race descent, many of them from the nation's biggest cities, leave behind their streetwise ways to become what were known as the "honorable workers" whom more and more teams were paying to play.[9] Today, the narrative would have a Brazilian footballer of humble background "rise" in the world to achieve fame, fortune, and image rights, in all probability playing his game somewhere other than his birthplace.

DaMatta's "destiny" may or may not be against CAM's players, but the "desire" they possess in their own heads, hearts, legs, and feet presumably must help them decide which way a given match can turn. Perhaps we might construe raça, then, as *mineiros'* way not of cheating fate but of placing it under the pressure of a fully committed, wholehearted style of play that Atlético has made its namesake. With roughly one-third of Latin America's population and about 40 percent of its GDP, Brazil today stands poised to overtake Great Britain and France to become the fifth-largest economy in the world. At the same time, such cultural traditions in Brazil as *jeitinho*, the informal network of relationships and favors that helps the well-positioned members of society bend the rules to their advantage, have not exactly made the nation a bastion of ethical business practices, or what we might call "a level playing field."[10] It stands to reason that the county's distribution of wealth should remain sharply divided under these circumstances. Much controversy nevertheless continues to attend governmental social programs in Brazil, such as Bolsa Família, which provides conditional cash transfers to poor families in a country where some people are barely able to subsist.[11] Raça wouldn't qualify as a means of redistributing Atlético's riches, but it could be interpreted as a form of futebol that bends the rules *back* in such a way that sheer human desire once again bears some influence on the outcomes of games on and off the pitch. This grit isn't in answer to graft, necessarily, but as a partial solution to problems of equity, opportunity, and endeavor that pervade Brazilian sport and society alike. Raça, in short, when posited as a component of CAM's play, could be seen as an embodied expression of the club's strenuous dedication to *work*. And the reward that the players who subscribe to this ethic receive in return for their more-than-ordinary level of effort at play is the promise of self-invention in a society where some combination of paternalism, "personalism," luck, and laissez-faire still shapes the prospects of so many.[12]

Raça e Raça

Raça may ultimately be a sign of "Blackness" more than a regional indicator of pluck. For of all the factors that have defined the contours of Brazilian life from the colonial period forward, perhaps none exceeds the influence of race in determining a person's place in the sporting and social orders. Indeed, in assessing the condition of the Black diaspora in the early 1950s, the French West Indian political philosopher Frantz Fanon would write, "However painful it may be for me to accept this conclusion, I am obliged to state it: For the black man there is only one destiny. And it is white."[13] Fanon has already predecided the winner in the contest between DaMatta's destiny and desire; for the Black man who was compelled to perform "White-ness" in what Fanon construes as a white man's world, Blackness precludes the possibility of a person's determining the trajectory of his or her life on his or her own terms. The legacy of Brazil's vexed racial history does not need to be recounted here to prove or disprove Fanon's thesis. As the last country in the Western Hemisphere to abolish slavery, which it belatedly did in 1888, Brazil has long grappled with sensitive questions of race and belonging in a society for which the label "multiethnic" barely suffices. Not only has futebol been implicated in Brazilians' ongoing discussions about the role that race plays in describing the arc of its citizens' lives; it has arguably been the foundation upon which the superstructure of its modern society has been built in response to the prevailing fact that is football.

Etymologically speaking, raça e raça share a linguistic lineage that belies the semantic divergence the two terms have taken in Brazilians' everyday speech. Among the players for Atlético with whom I spoke, none was prepared to draw a line of meaningful connection between the congruence of two words that, from the perspective of a white outsider who was perhaps too eager to draw conclusions from idiomatic coincidence, might help explain an emotion that few would deny but no one could define. What Stuart Hall calls the "floating signifier" of race nevertheless shadows the contradictory meanings of raça. Indeed, these meanings have no more afforded mineiros what Hall describes as a "foundational guarantee" in their "classificatory systems of difference" than has the illusory *political* prospect that racial difference itself can somehow be shown to be "biologically constituted" and thus destined.[14] More than circumstantial evidence would appear to link the politics of race and the politics of raça, regardless. And it was not long before I found myself thinking of this suggestive overlap as further proof, perhaps, of the capacity of a modern sports establishment that's become closely identified with the Black athlete for demonstrating what Ben Carrington names *"the political nature of the apolitical."*[15] In the landmark article "Foot-ball mulato" that he wrote in 1938 for the newspaper *Diários Associados*, Brazilian social scientist Gilberto Freyre proposes what would become a sustaining myth of the country's favorite sport (and, by extension, its national identity) well into the twentieth century.[16] Comparing the unstudied artistry of Brazil's mixed-race players, who were only then beginning to gain a more conspicuous presence in the domestic game, with the comparative predictableness and "geometrical" rationalism of Europe's white footballers, Freyre conflates what he sees as the racialized traits of *"mulatos"* with the free-flowing form of futebol they played when given the opportunity, as they were in the two matches against French sides Strasbourg and Bourdeaux that precipitated Freyre's commentary. Freyre characterizes what he calls *"mulatismo"* as a set of in-born qualities best expressed by a person who's "agile in assimilating, dominating, light-footed in dance."[17] As for the football that persons of mixed ethnicity and a range of darker skin tones played, Freyre would have us believe that this sport is full of "surprise, guile, cunning, lightness and at the same time individual spontaneity" (4). What Freyre suggests is that people of certain racial characteristics are given to playing the game a certain way—or, rather more immoderately, Freyre is prepared to use the racial (il)logic of his hypothesis as the basis for a far more sweeping claim: "Psychologically," he declares, "being a Brazilian is being mulatto" (4). By such grandiose standards, the related proposition (which I am by no means endorsing) that Black players might play the game with more raça than others seems modest, but it, too, finally amounts to little more than racial stereotyping. These stereotypes help explain why more and more Brazilian clubs began to enlist Black players into their squads during a period following de facto segregation in the 1930s and 1940s, such that the storied sports journalist Mário Filho could write, in his still-read postwar book *O negro no futebol Brasileiro* (1947), that people were living in what he names "*A Vez do Preto*" (The Time of Blacks).[18]

Filho's pronouncement at best describes an aspirational racial dynamic. At the turn of the twentieth century, many of the country's most privileged white people promulgated an idea of "whitening" Brazilian society, such that the nation's African and Indigenous blood lines would be diffused though a process of miscegenation that would eventually remake the nation according to what was perceived to be a "European" pattern of shared identity. This gesture was not a sign of noblesse oblige by whites; rather, it was an attempt carried out by the self-regarding members of a racial minority to remake Black folk and *mestiços* in their own image. When white elites acknowledged peoples of color at all, they tended to view them as undisciplined and improvidently free-spirited, forever looking for diversion, but never ready to *work*.[19]

What followed over the course of the next several decades in Brazil was a period of intensified nationalism and anti-monarchical complaint, and the cultural environment that emerged in these years ironically grew more and more receptive than before to the nation's everyday expressions of "Blackness," which came to be seen as what two recent observers have called a "ludic" means of reconciling racial difference and unifying a fully modernized Brazil through "play."[20] Freyre's *mulatismo* enjoyed enhanced favor in these years as the domestic popularity of samba, *carnaval*, and futebol soared. This observation is not to suggest that an easy racial harmony ensued. Noticeable setbacks occurred, most memorably in 1950, when a vocal contingent of the press and public sought to attribute Brazil's humiliating home loss to Uruguay in the World Cup (the most coveted prize in world football for qualifying national teams) to the underperformance of three Black players, one of whom, left back João Ferreira, or Bigode ("moustache" in Portuguese), was a native of Belo Horizonte and had begun his club career playing with Atlético Mineiro from 1940 to 1943.[21] Brazil's run of World Cup successes in 1958, 1962, and 1970 would somewhat ease racial tensions in the country, thanks in no small part to the vital contributions of such "Black" players as Pelé and Garrincha, who was part Black and part Fulnio. Well into the current century, however, Brazil has continued to parse the meaning of "play" by attending to the racial overtones of its preferred sport. Witness the remarks made by the Afro-Brazilian philosopher, writer, and activist Sueli Carneiro when she complained during a televised interview with rapper Mano Brown in May 2022 that Black footballers were purposefully being excluded from the game. Carneiro was speaking on this occasion to what she called "the whitening of Brazilian football," a retrograde development that she tied directly to the discriminatory practices that she alleged have been denying Blacks access to the game at all levels, from recreational to professional.[22] Writing about the perilous (yet potentially liberating) relationship between society and sport in the United States under COVID-19, Grant Farred captures the racial tenor of Carneiro's concerns in the title of his 2022 book, *Only a Black Athlete Can Save Us Now*.[23] Carneiro might second Farred's emotions if only there were, by her count, any Black footballers still playing in Brazil.

That any futebol club, CAM included, should lay claim to raça as something worth wanting within the context of Brazil's conflicted racial history might seem surprising, but there are reasons— some of them witting, some not—why they would do so. From at least the 1930s, sports columnists in Brazil have been using the most positive connotations of the term *raça* for patriotic purposes, as when the country's oldest daily sports newspaper, the Rio de Janeiro–based *Jornal dos Sports*, hailed "the strength" of the "privileged race of strong men" who claimed the South American rowing championships for their country in March 1931.[24] Raça in this instance not only was applied to a sport other than football but was meant to denominate a "race" of Brazilians in emphatically nationalist rather than narrowly ethnic terms.

Then again, rowing, not football, was the most popular sport in Rio de Janeiro at the turn of the twentieth century. And although several sports associations in the city, most notably Clube de Regatas do Flamengo, would eventually combine rowing with football as the appeal of the latter sport grew, their constituents remained predominantly white. As a key to raça's range of contemporary usage, in any case, *Jornal dos Sports*'s lexical register was far more accommodating than the admissions policies of Rio's regatta clubs.

To begin, the paper applied the label raça liberally (but not too liberally) to athletes from a range of sports, including football, boxing, and even cricket. One looks in vain in these early years, however, for a Black footballer—or a Black athlete of any kind, really—being described as *raçudo*, meaning that he was regarded by commentators as "having" raça. Yet there are instances of (white) French boxers being described as having raça, and there are references as well to a *"raça Latina"* and a *"raça Negra."*[25] Thus, even a cursory examination of the then-current racial discourse in Brazil during the first half of the twentieth century would suggest that the sports-related inflections of raça were either a desirable thing or a relatively neutral thing, but probably not a "Black" thing.

That would begin to change in much the same way that *mulatismo* evolved in Brazil from carrying a stigma of racial inferiority to being an exciting signifier of ethnic *raciness*. If raça was once the exclusive preserve of white people, it soon came to apply to increasing numbers of Black athletes as their performances before an admiring sports public earned them the respect that was their due. The consensual understanding of raça accordingly expanded just enough to quietly admit Black footballers because of their ability to *play*. Sometime Brazilian midfielder Didi, for example, retired by this stage in his illustrious career but back home in Rio de Janeiro to celebrate *carnaval*, made a cameo appearance in the pages of *Jornal dos Sports* in January 1968 with the *"raça"* of a *"sambista."*[26] Another class act in these years was the entire Rio de Janeiro side Vasco da Gama, with a multiracial squad that *Jornal* praised for using raça to impose its technical superiority on opponents who resorted to a violent style of play to offset their deficiencies.[27] But, as we have seen, raça contains feelings of many shades, so it was quite feasible that teams depending on *violência* and other negative tactics might themselves be recognized for fielding players with *raçudo*, regardless of their race.[28] Indeed, raça had been loosened up enough by the late 1960s that the traditional racial profiles of Black and white players might be reversed. This switch is exactly what happened when *Jornal* ran a feature article in April 1968 describing the impact that the *"alegria"* of Vasco's white midfielder Adílson had had on his team's raça; by contrast, the paper called it an "irony of destiny" (*ironia do destino*) that Mário, a darker-skinned and "embittered" (*amargurado*) player for Vasco's most recent vanquished opponent, Bangu, should show great "tranquility" of "temperament" in a loss that he called "one of the most unfair I've suffered in my career."[29] Raça might not have become the sole possession of Black athletes, but it was no longer monopolized by whites.

Mário's disappointments notwithstanding, we might say that Blackness by this time represented a far greater range of emotions in Brazil than it ever had before. Whether it signified the "bitterness" of defeat or the unrelenting bite of raça, the buoyancy of spontaneity or the "tranquility" of the professional athlete who'd seen it all before, Black ceased to be the most reductive of racial signs in a country (like many others, including my own) that had long made race a convenient shorthand for the perpetuation of all manner of prejudice. Black even began to make claims to being "beautiful" in Brazil by the 1970s. As a social movement, "Black Is Beautiful" had, of course, emerged in the United States during the previous decade under the leadership of a pan-Africanist cohort of activist African Americans. And with the international spread of the movement's message, a small group of like-minded residents in Rio de Janeiro would be advocating locally for a short-lived equivalent of "Black Is Beautiful" by August 1976, when a photo shoot appearing in the prominent Rio daily *Jornal do Brasil* sparked controversy with its images of Black men sporting afros and platform shoes.[30] Not everyone in the country was offended by what some critics cited as evidence of "unBrazilian" behavior. In fact, *Jornal dos Sports* had anticipated Brazil's fleeting "Black Is Beautiful" moment five years earlier when it published interviews with four of domestic football's Black *craques*, or star players, under the attention-grabbing headline "*Negros Podem Ser Brancos*" (Blacks Can Be Whites). The premise for the piece was the growing fad for the elective procedure by which Black clients in the United States and abroad were paying to have their skin whitened. Asked by journalist Marilene Dabus (the first woman to cover football in Brazil) how they felt about these procedures, the assembled cast of standout footballers voiced an unmistakable pride in their race. Acknowledging that "*racismo existe no Brasil*," Paulo César, or "Caju," as he was commonly known, re-marked, "It is difficult for a Negro to excel in his profession." Right winger Jairzinho was concerned less with immediate questions of *work* than the larger existential implications of what he effectively likened to an act of self-negation, saying, "If they [those who under-went skin-whitening] change color it is because they are ashamed of being black. I find this absurd." Goalkeeper Ubirajara framed the problem in economic terms, pointing out that if a wealthy "Creole" were Black, Brazilians at worst were prepared to look upon him as "navy blue." And as for the Minas Gerais native Fio Maravilha, the very gesture of a Black person lightening his skin color no longer made sense, he said, "now that race has morals" (*agora que a raça está com moral*). Maravilha's contention might well stand for those of the rest of *Jornal*'s interviewees. By July 1971, when the paper conducted these conversations—and some five months before CAM secured the title of Brazil's newly formed Brasileirão—the best Black players in the country were ready to lay claim to more raça, not less, in every sense of the word.[31]

CAM necessarily confronted these questions alongside other teams in the new league, but with a critical difference. With his full-fledged Atlético debut in 1973, CAM's legendary *artilheiro*, striker José Reinaldo de Lima, known as "Reinaldo," would make raça an all but unavoidable topic of conversation in a nation that often regarded those who broached issues of race as agitators. His-torian Roger Kittleson calls Reinaldo "another rebellious craque," and with good reason.[32] The upraised fist that Reinaldo used to celebrate his goals during the latter part of the decade, especially, paid obvious tribute to two African American athletes, Tommie Smith and John Carlos, who had earlier shocked the world with the Black Power salute they gave after receiving their track-and-field medals at the 1968 Olympics in Mexico City (Figure 2.1). Rein-aldo's youth (he was a mere teenager when he became a first-team regular with Atlético) and boyish, photogenic appearance might have taken a bit of the edge off the player's politics, but the goal-scorer whom the Brazilian press had begun to call "Baby-Craque" pulled no punches when he asserted himself on and off the field. Philipe Van R. Lima, Reinaldo's son and biographer, dwells on

Figure 2.1 Clube Atlético Mineiro striker Reinaldo, his fist raised after scoring one of his 255 goals for CAM. (*Photograph by Delfim Vieira.*)

what he describes as the "coolness and tranquility" with which his father finished scoring opportunities when he played.[33] For all the feelings he inspired in supporters, *o Rei* was always in control of his own emotions, despite the relentless pressure he faced as defenders corralled, kicked, and pushed CAM's ace up and down the length of the pitch since they could find no other way to contain him. Lima writes that to this extent, Reinaldo "embodied the spirit of the team," a claim with which even non-atleticanos were inclined to agree when they considered the player's larger body of work (51). An editorial appearing in *Jornal dos Sports* in April 1977, for example, spoke at once to the "common sense," "lucidity," and "good deportment" with which the rebel Reinaldo played. Without ever using the word *raça* to characterize the performances of the player, the author of these "confidential" remarks perhaps paid Reinaldo the highest compliment of all when he honored him for the "certain didactic force" in his style of play. Reinaldo had not only helped make raça righteous; he carried himself in such a way that his manner of playing became instructive for those who were fortunate enough to watch.[34]

It would be hard to imagine the current incarnation of CAM without accounting for the impact Reinaldo had on the *alvinegro*. These were my feelings before sitting down to talk with the striker, and they remain my sentiments to this day. Our meeting took place at noon on a Friday in early June 2022, at Belo Horizonte's Palácio das Mangabeiras. Named after the flowering, fruit-bearing plant of the same name—and not the newspaper cartoonist Fernando Pierucetti, who, under the pseudonym "Mangabeira," was invited by the daily *A Folha de Minas* to create the mascots for Belo Horizonte's three biggest football teams in 1945—the palace served until recently as the official governor's mansion for Minas Gerais state. The self-made Brazilian businessman who occupied the aforementioned political office at the time of my writing was Romeu Zema, who thought it better to vacate the residence so that its leafy grounds could be used as a public park on the days of its designated openings. The governor's erstwhile *palácio* was closed to visitors on the day I met *o Rei* there. Joining him were his son Lima as well as his friend Peter Eriksson, the Canadian honorary consul to Belo Horizonte who trained with Reinaldo as a professional footballer at CAM in the late 1980s and early 1990s. Joining (and driving) me was my colleague at Universidade Federal de Minas Gerais (UFMG) Luciana Fiuza, who had arranged the interview with Reinaldo's personal assistant. The first and last order of business as our proceedings got underway was a discussion of raça.

Like his former teammate Nelinho, Reinaldo mostly thought of raça as "instinctive." He described it as "a physical disposition that's something natural to the player," even though, he pointed out, raça also has "emotional and psychological" aspects that we need to take stock of if we want to understand the nuances of the game. I inquired about any racial or ethnic components to raça, and Reinaldo demurred. He did, however, admit that raça was not entirely congenital. Rather, "You have to nurture raça as a player," he explained, so that even in training, players "have to summon something extra to be a little more aggressive." This comment is not to say that Reinaldo (or anyone else present) was ready to liken raça to simple "fight" or "tenacity." "Football *is* a fight; it's a manly game," Reinaldo continued. "You have to overcome everything with raça." But raça couldn't be thought of independently from amor, he cautioned, since it was finally "love" for which an Atlético Mineiro player was fighting. The one and only stipulation of raça from Reinaldo's perspective was this: "Defend your love with all your guts." It was a prescription with which another of CAM's cognoscenti, the sometime football broadcaster Bolivar, would no doubt agree.[35]

As our conversation unfolded high in the hilltops of Belo Horizonte, I could feel race beginning to fall out of the equation that I'd been formulating in my mind to better appreciate raça. Contrary feelings pulled me in the opposite direction as well. I still needed to consider the question of COVID-19, for starters. Sitting and talking (without a mask) with a small group of people who, by all appearances, were doing just fine, medically speaking, I had to remind myself that people of color were disproportionately affected by the coronavirus here, much as they were elsewhere in the hemisphere. Indeed, during the worst of the pandemic, the Black population of Minas Gerais suffered from a 46 percent higher mortality rate from COVID-19 than did any other sector of the state's population.[36] Reinaldo himself said that the first wave of the coronavirus had been "a moment of emptiness for Atlético supporters," without whom raça persisted but was "invisible" inside Atlético's empty stadium.[37]

CAM may have since recovered from the strains of COVID-19, but it has a complex history that intersects with questions of race in myriad other ways. The illustrator Mangabeira, it should be noted, is said to have based his image of Galo on a black-and-white species of rooster, *Galo Carijó*, that was known in Belo Horizonte in the early part of the twentieth century as a fiercely competitive gamecock in the cockfights that many mixed-race spectators patronized as they partook of the city's vernacular entertainments. Then, too, the martial airs of the Clube's original anthem from 1928 likewise gave way to the racially encoded rhythmic swing of Mota's samba-influenced *hino*, or hymn, from 1969.[38] Whether or not CAM's fans realize it, there is something "racial" in the main song they sing during matches to help players *dar raça*, to *give* raça. The same racial claims could be made more generally about the open emotional displays and thumping musical accompaniment of

Figure 2.2 Standing room only among the *torcida*. (*Photograph by Eugênio Sávio. Courtesy Clube Atlético Mineiro.*)

the *charanga* bands that are now a mainstay of the *torcida* (meaning "to cheer" or "to twist") supporters' groups, such as Galoucura (translation: Galo "madness"), Resistência, Inferno, and Galö Metal, that enliven CAM's home and away matches today (Figure 2.2). As paying Black supporters began to be admitted into football matches in Brazil in the 1920s and 1930s, the conventional genteel discipline of such crowd reactions as handkerchief-waving and polite applause that had previously made these whites-only gatherings somewhat staid and colorless affairs slackened enough to make *twisting* and *shouting* an acceptable affective response to sport.[39] Much to Reinaldo's point about the accepted means of fostering a culture of raça at CAM, moreover, many of the players from an earlier generation were also able to *learn* some version of raça after Black footballers in the 1930s began to emulate the gamesmanship and rough-and-tumble "European" style of play that was being waged against them by white players. For the earliest Black footballers in Brazil, fighting back was a question of adapting or dying, and such was the success of their seeming "assimilation" that we well might forget that their collective decision to no longer turn the other cheek had as much to do with a basic need for self-preservation as it did with raça.

Reinaldo took care to remind me that Americans often don't enjoy games like futebol, which can end in a draw. We prefer to have a clear winner in our athletic contests, he said, and he's not wrong. But as a man who endured more abuse on the playing field than most, Reinaldo recognized as well that raça, whatever else it might mean, connotes a dignified means of keeping oneself and one's team alive, of remaining in a match no matter how unfavorable the sporting (or not) conditions might be. In this regard, Reinaldo remembered times when he would conserve his stores of raça during matches for those moments when he needed it most. Perhaps this mentality was what the fans of Galo were referring to when they released a video on YouTube in 2013 chronicling their backs-to-the-wall, come-from-behind success in the 2013 edition of South America's Copa Libertadores. With a nod to the one and only Black U.S. president, Barack Obama, Galo let everyone know, "Yes We C.A.M."[40]

Raça de Dia, Raça à Noite

The first Atlético match that I attended in person was a night game, the home draw against São Paulo's Santos on Saturday, June 11, 2022. Streaming the matches of the Brasileirão on Paramount+ in the United States does not prepare a person for the galvanizing experience of a live viewing in Brazil.[41] Then again, this observation would be true for any sport, in any country. But surrounded as I was by some twenty-six thousand supporters (most of them enlisted with CAM) willing their side to victory, I was obtaining a clearer sense of what raça means in real time. Reinaldo had not just been diplomatic when he spoke of the torcida as "the twelfth man" whose "presence is fundamental to the game."[42] The effect that A Massa has on the quality of play on the pitch becomes palpable when you are there to witness it gathered in full force. The singing of the songs, the beating of the drums, the uncensored exclamations that pour forth from the mouths of fans toward the action em campo, on the field, all immerse a person in the call-and-response of emotions that pervade the Mineirão on matchdays. It is easier to appreciate that raça is real when you *feel* it en masse among Galo's supporters. Never mind that I appeared to have been the only person in the stadium wearing a COVID mask.

This allowance for the impact of the torcida on the game was not the only adjustment that I needed to make to my views on raça after I watched Atlético's players perform right in front of me: There was also the matter of *work* to which I had to attend. In their warmups before the match, the players went through their usual preparations like the professionals they are. These occurred at half-speed at best, there being no need for the starters, especially, to tire themselves before the match kicked off at 7:00 P.M. local time. When play did begin, the players went to work, as Reinaldo had told me they would. "The job is unpredictable," he'd said. A player may not be "inspired" on any given day. He may be injured. He could be dealing with family problems at home. Yet "like every worker," Reinaldo assured me, each player had a "responsibility" to himself and the Clube to give everything he had to the match once his shift started with the sound of the official's whistle. In the game against Santos, CAM's entire squad was on the front foot right from the offing, their energy levels and enthusiasm finding an objective correlative in the quickened pulse of the torcida. Atlético's starting eleven passed with precision. They tackled with purpose. They chased down every ball, even the lost causes. And save for some lax defending from time to time (as champions from the previous season, Atlético's 2022 side showed a decided preference for the attacking side of the game), CAM's players provided every indication that they were anything but complacent. This match, on this night, would not decide itself. Atlético was there to work *and* play.

What I can also say about raça after having stood within virtual touching distance of its expression is that it's revisionist. Granted, my vantage from the "cheap" seats in the upper decks of the Mineirão (in the "red" portion of the stadium, designated *vermelho superior*) was not the best. Yet the emotional context that surrounded this specific match and that lent it special significance did not require optimum sight lines for me and my atleticana companions Luciana and Elaine. Our view was wholly unobstructed, in any case, and afforded me a perspective on the action for which I would have expected to pay dearly had I been attending a comparable sporting event in the United States. Coming into the match, CAM was emerging from what had been the team's worst loss under new manager Antonio Mohamed, who had taken over for Cuca in January 2022. Indeed, after playing thirty-two games under Mohamed, a former Argentine international whose combined Lebanese, Syrian, and Croatian descent explains his Spanish nickname, *El Turco* (The Turk), Atlético had never conceded more than two goals. Yet in the midweek away match against the Rio de Janeiro side Fluminense on Wednesday, June 8, CAM had scored three but conceded an embarrassing five, a tally not equaled by the side in eleven years. This result was unacceptable by the standards of the players and supporters alike.

As Mohamed explained in his postmatch press conference, Atlético's response was not to fixate on the past but to control what it could in the present—that is, to concentrate on the next match. In the manager's words, "We hope to correct all errors and on Saturday return to our identity. That's what we have to do: recover our identity and play as a great team, which doesn't concede as many goals."[43] Mohamed furthermore accepted responsibility for the poor showing, saying that the team's defensive frailties were a reflection of his own shortcomings in planning for the match. But no matter how we might account for the loss, the manager's retrospective musings highlight for us an essential dimension of raça that we have already seen. Rather than defer to destiny, the Clube's players believed that their desire to set things right would produce an entirely different outcome on Saturday. This attitude is normal; it's perhaps inevitable, given CAM's crowded fixture list. And still, despite Atlético's concession of a late penalty against ten-man Santos in its subsequent match, a game in which the home side dominated ball possession against a mid-table opponent, the manner by which the team had readied itself for rehabilitation almost immediately after its last defeat recalled for me what the eponymous narrator from nineteenth-century Brazilian author Machado de Assis's novel *Memorías póstumas de Brás Cubas* (1880) named his "Theory of Human Editions." As the titular hero Brás relates, our lives will always be "full of errata and barbarisms" and thus need to be "revised and amended."[44] But the beauty of any literary conception of our existence that's *game* (and the brash, devil-may-care narrator Brás is nothing if not a player) is precisely that it affords us repeated opportunities for correcting our imperfections in the here and now. Many of the fans who surrounded me on Saturday night left the Mineirão disappointed. They were interested less in the ongoing revision of their Clube's living history than they were in the forgetfulness that awaited them at the local bars and the many food carts jammed together outside the stadium, offering mineiro versions of a Brazilian dish best served warm, *feijão tropeiro*. Perhaps the supporters had a point. The 1–1 scoreline probably was a fair result when we consider that Santos tested CAM's goalkeeper Éverson on several occasions, even before having one of their players shown a red card in the sixtieth minute.

To focus on the result alone, however, is to overlook the way that raça had set the tone for the match from the very beginning. CAM came at Santos with wave after wave of attacking pressure in the opening minutes, exploiting the right side of the Santos defense to achieve a clear competitive advantage. In fact, a well-placed cross from Atlético's left side of the field allowed Sávio to open the scoring for the home side in the sixth minute, and CAM continued to press for the next twenty minutes or so, perhaps running ragged in the process. Even with the game waning deep into second-half injury time, however, the team never ceased to compete with a determination that had more than a hint of "fight" about it. Wednesday's match against Fluminense had been a disaster, and the time for rewriting that poor showing was now, in raça's ever-present tense. Situated as it is within a temporal setting of regularly recurring "festivals," whether these be the World Cups staged every four years at the international level or the annual domestic league championships that are played by professional teams year after year, football depends upon an assumed recurrence that is hospitable to raça.[45] Without the possibility of revision, there would be no need to play the games at all. But since revision is the organizing principle of football as a sport, a club like Atlético Mineiro can have a manager like Mohamed, who played his inadvertent part, as boss of the Tijuana side from Mexico that Atlético beat at the quarter-final stage of its triumphant run to the Copa Libertadores title, in writing CAM's storied history.[46] And with an away game against the northeastern Brazilian side Ceará still to come on the following Wednesday before its players faced their traditional foes Flamengo at home on Sunday, in a much anticipated contest, Atlético retained the right to tell its own story, in its own way, when the team again took to the pitch. Destiny had nothing to do with it.

Not even Atlético Mineiro can summon a victory whenever it wants, no more than the rest of us can satisfy all our desires through wishing and working. Wednesday night's fixture at the Arena Castelão duly ended in a goalless stalemate, with neither side ever looking likely to score. If that were not enough of an anticlimax ahead of Sunday's kickoff at 4:00 P.M. against Flamengo, then there was also the news from Thursday of the murder in the Amazon of British journalist (and sometime football writer) Dom Phillips, who had been researching a book on the depredations made against Brazil's rainforests by the region's miners, ranchers, and fishermen.[47] Such was the emotional blow of the latter tragedy that it prompted CAM's best-known current chronicler, journalist Fred Melo Paiva, to write in his weekly column for the *Jornal Estado de Minas*, "This was one of those weeks . . . when you have the feeling that football should stop." Paiva wasn't simply referring to Atlético Mineiro's four straight matches without a victory; his remarks carried a more sweeping environmental import, as the reporter lamented his country's larger losses, stating, "And we all died together from this disease called Brazil."[48] These words were sobering, to be sure.

My spirits were already low as the matchday with Flamengo approached, for reasons far less honorable than anything Phillips had stood for in his work. I might have been lucky enough to stroll the landscaped grounds of Palácio das Mangabeiras with footballing royalty, but fortune had not favored my efforts to secure tickets for the weekend's big match, which proved unobtainable. Nor had I had foresight enough to plan something festive for the business end of the holiday season, June in Brazil hosting the weeks-long *Festa Junina* celebrations that combine a succession of Catholic saints' days with harvest-time tributes to a variety of traditional foods, drinks, and folkways. I instead had to make do with watching Galo at home on Globo TV. To make matters worse, I was beginning to earn a reputation around the UFMG campus for having *pé frio*, or cold feet. No one there had accused me outright of bringing bad luck ("cold feet" in Portuguese means "lacking good fortune") to Atlético Mineiro in the form of my interloper's support for the side, but people intimated that my *pé* were at best what one wag in the Office of International Relations described as *morno*, meaning "lukewarm." I suppose that I might have taken this characterization as a compliment of sorts, since much the same had been said of Mick Jagger, of the Rolling Stones, after he attended Brazil's crushing 7–1 home defeat (in Belo Horizonte, no less) to Germany in the semifinals of the 2014 World Cup.[49] All things being equal, which they seldom are, I'm sure that I would have rather had my feet be *quente*.

As it turned out, CAM didn't need my personal fortunes to turn for the team to be "reborn," as a writer for the online Brazilian sports journal *The Lance!* stated.[50] The match itself was not a matter of life and death, but stirrings leading into the contest had suggested that Turco Mohamed's head might roll unless results improved in the short term—and improve they did. The fixture began with both sides engaging in some sloppy play. A misplaced pass here, players literally taking their eyes off the ball there—it was a less than inspiring display for the first ten minutes or so, in front of a full house (*casa cheia*) that was making its collective voice heard. Once Atlético's players gathered themselves, however, they were never unduly troubled by a Flamengo side whose low standing in the league table accurately reflected the overall state of their play thirteen matches into the season. CAM came to dictate play as the first half unfolded, until the game's standout performer, the Argentine midfielder Nacho Fernández, finished off a flicked-on header by teammate Keno to open the scoring in the thirty-fifth minute. The sense of relief that must have been felt inside the stadium was transmitted all the way to my modish studio apartment, located some 8.7 kilometers away, near the city center. Atlético's supporters erupted, the players celebrated, and the Clube's technical staff reacted as if they'd just received a stay of execution. It was, admittedly, hard to think about raça amid this congeries of emotions. Yet it would be fair to say on the strength of this overall performance that Atlético Mineiro's squad had taken to the pitch with no intention of yielding to the visitors from Rio de Janeiro. And when CAM's Ademir kept his composure to double the home side's advantage five minutes before the end of regulation, his low strike from twelve yards out finding the bottom-right-hand corner of Flamengo's net, Galo crowed like it hadn't crowed in some weeks' time. Raça or not, to paraphrase Gertrude Stein, a win is a win is a win.[51]

Talking Raça, or the Players' Perspective

Having begun and ended his professional career at CAM, making the most all-time appearances for the Clube—684—during his playing days in the 1970s, 1980s, and 1990s, goalkeeper João Leite is as well positioned as anyone to talk about raça. As a state deputy in the Assembleia Legislativa de Minas Gerais since 1995, representing the Brazilian Social Democracy Party (PSDB), Leite might also be considered a professional talker of sorts. That said, we did not talk politics when I met him at his offices in August—we talked sport.

The key to understanding an "intangible" emotion like raça, Leite told me, is the supporters. He explained that raça is a "passion," a "fire," and that unless the players were "inflamed" by the fans in the stands, they would not be able to play with any "heart."[52] It all sounded a little like alchemy to me. A feeling that we were describing as a "fire" from within relied upon the spark of an external source from without; "passion" as such was something a person couldn't have unless he or she entered a mutually sustaining relation with someone else who did. We might as well have been talking about loving when we were supposed to be talking about fighting. It turns out that we were talking about religion. As a native of a high and dry northern region of Minas Gerais, Vale do Jequitinhonha, João himself was a supporter of CAM as a child. But despite what he describes in his self-published autobiography as "my childhood joys and professional achievement in football," he writes, "there was in my heart, in my thoughts, a very great fear of death."[53] This fear occurred long before the perils of COVID-19 appeared in the new millennium, mind you. Leite's fears of his own mortality were of a spiritual nature and brought him to dedicate his game to God and his personal "Salvador," Jesus Cristo, while he also began to proselytize among players in the 1980s and 1990s as the main force behind the *Atletas de Cristo* evangelical Christian movement (63). I refrained from asking Leite whether Jesus had raça, even after the player explained that he himself had shown that emotion during his playing days mostly through the suffering he did on behalf of his team and teammates. In other words, Leite played through the pain of an athlete's chronic injuries; his passion, or *paixão*, manifested not in his time upon any cross but in the minutes that this strapping mountain of a man recorded between "the sticks" as a goalkeeper, as the representatives of that informal union say. Known while he was still an active player as *Goleiro de Deus* (God's Goalkeeper), Leite made it part of his "mission" to hand out Bibles to opposing players. There is no recorded instance of him ever giving away a goal.

The first meeting of Leite's religious movement—and it is a full-fledged movement—drew just four players, including our goalkeeper. Membership in *Atletas de Cristo* has since climbed to seven thousand players in sixty different countries, including such influential members of the Brazilian futebol community as stars Neymar and Rivaldo.[54] This alteration of the sporting landscape is to be expected in a place like Brazil; since the time when Leite devoted himself to the work of conversion in 1980, the number of evangelical Christians there had risen from 6.6 percent of the total population to 31 percent in 2021. It is even expected that evangelicals will outnumber a once-dominant Catholic stronghold of worshippers by 2032, meaning that it will be no easier in Minas to bar players from holding religious revival meetings in hotels and locker rooms—as has become an occasional practice with the Brazilian national team—than it is in other regions of this vast nation, where such African-influenced syncretic religions as candomblé also contribute to the heterogeneous quality of a politically contested cultural life.[55]

Leite reflected fondly on his early days at Atlético Mineiro, when the Clube's championship-winning coach Telê Santana had insisted that players from the side's youth and juvenile teams be given regular opportunities to train with the senior squad. Leite believes that this attitude is how raça was once cultivated at CAM, during a time when, in his opinion, raça e amor reached their historical peak.[56] It is hard to say whether the peace and love promulgated by those with Protestant evangelical leanings are being instilled in players behind the scenes at Atlético Mineiro today, in combination with the raça that has long been the Clube's secular religion. It is worth noting that the largest Pentecostal church in the state of Minas Gerais, belonging to the *Igreja Universal do Reino de Deus*, sits in the Lourdes neighborhood of Belo Horizonte, a few short blocks from CAM's headquarters.[57]

Defensive midfielder Rafael Miranda was also prepared to look upon raça from a more holistic point of view than most, situating it within the context of his relationship not to God but to his grandmother. Born in Belo Horizonte ("I was always a supporter of the club," he told me), Miranda was attending CAM's matches at the Mineirão with his father by the time he was two years old. His return trip there as a player began in 1993, when he joined the Clube's *futsal* team, or what Americans would call "indoor soccer." A coach at CAM's youth setup asked him only a few years later to enter "the system," and Miranda would make his debut with the first team in 2003 at age eighteen before returning to the academy for more seasoning. He played some additional top-flight games in 2005, the year that CAM was relegated to Campeonato Brasileiro Série B, before finally settling into the side during the Série B season of 2006 that saw the Clube promoted once again to Brazil's Série A.

None of which explains why Miranda is still known in Minas Gerais as *Xodó da Vovó*, a phrase that loosely translates as "granny's boy." The player received this *nom de game* from the announcer at a popular radio station in Belo Horizonte the day after newspaper headlines there enshrined the circumstances of Rafael's scoring his first goal for the Clube. Days before the match in question, Miranda's grandmother had made a surprise appearance at the Cidade do Galo training facility to visit her grandson.

Answering questions from the press after she arrived, she had said that Rafael would score his first goal for Atlético at the upcoming match. Sure enough, Miranda did score in the thirteenth minute of that next game, dedicating the goal to his grandmother for good measure. It all sounded so sweet, until I asked the player about raça. He paused thoughtfully when I introduced the topic, telling me, "It's such a common word for us that it's hard to imagine a person who doesn't know what it means."[58] Nonetheless, he ventured an explanation for his stubbornly insistent American interlocutor that began with his providing the requisite alternatives for a word that has no exact equivalent in English: "Determination" and "dedication" were his preferred terms. As for whether raça could be taught, Miranda responded, "You *choose* to have it. It's not something you're born to." Considering that he played in the 2006 side that was tasked with fighting its way back into the first division, Miranda might have said that raça's reputedly elective quality was favorable for the players, since the lower futebol leagues in Brazil, in Rafael's telling, feature a less "technical" game that calls for even more raça than the comparatively silky-smooth play of Série A.[59] What most distinguished Miranda's views on "fight" in football are as follows, however. First, he regarded raça not as a feeling but as a *physical* condition that exists beyond what he referred to as the "psychological" dimensions of the game. He made this observation, I should relate, with all the animation of someone who presents anything but a flat affect. Our "granny's boy" furthermore told me this about raça: "It's about how you face your life, how you face all the challenges in your life." If Miranda believed these words—and I have every reason to suspect that he did, for he spoke to me with great feeling—then he also belied them, in that the extra emphasis he imparted to his observations suggested that he was someone who would go beyond the "limits" that so many players (Rafael included) had mentioned as raça's temperamental threshold.[60] To restrict our conceptualizations of raça to an affectless physical condition would mean in any case that we'd have to ignore the emotional implications behind Miranda's own insights about "fight" in futebol. Miranda had made his living in the game until as recently as 2018. At the time of our discussion in August 2022, he was confronting what he called "the challenges" in life beyond the pitch yet still reverting to raça to conjure up the kinds of personal traits that most of us would agree that we all need to make it through our days. After listening to Miranda talk with such intelligence, I guess that he was tapping into something more than "physical" in his life after futebol. By all appearances, he seemed to have been a thinker and a fighter as a professional player. As a football philosopher after the fact, he was now feeling his way toward something that not even the most self-aware of us can easily muster, what the literary scholar Kenneth Burke calls "equipment for living."[61] Rafael's grandmother, I should add, was doing just fine at age ninety-five when I spoke to him, even after testing positive for COVID-19 the month before.

At age thirty-seven, Atlético's center back Réver has been the standard-bearer for raça at the club he loves over the course of two separate spells with CAM. The first of these lasted from 2010 to 2014, when Réver earned the unofficial title "Captain America" while leading his side to its Copa Libertadores honors in 2013. The second is ongoing and began with the player's re-signing in 2019. Tall, strong, and unflappable in defense, Réver has contributed mightily to Atlético's extended stretch of high competitiveness during this period, and he remains a favorite with supporters even today, despite no longer being the first-choice option in the team's back line. The reasons for his continuing popularity are clear: A player who defines raça, in his own words, as "giving life on the pitch" could not have expended more of himself for the Clube than he already has.[62] Alive to the expectations of A Massa, Réver exerts himself to the full every time he takes to the pitch.

Like other Atlético players, Réver may be able to explain raça's reason for being—it's a "representation" of the feelings of the fans, he says—but he, too, professes less certainty about how raça comes to *be*. "The raça on the field happens from the moment you feel motivated and willing to do everything to win," Réver told me, in a statement that I might reduce to the enigmatic epigram "Raça happens."[63] What's not explained by the player's description here is the source of his own motivation. It would almost seem as if raça creeps up on him unaware, so that he's suddenly prepared to fight without knowing why. Or, rather, the game in which he finds himself playing demands that he be *racudo* (display raça), and his is not to reason why but to do and die, if need be. Réver's former teammate Victor, CAM's long-serving goalkeeper of the Libertadores years, could also account for raça's effects but not its causes. Victor described raça to me as a "kind of greater-than-usual willpower that goes towards overcoming" in "the pursuit of a result."[64] Here again, we have a "will" without a *why*.

As Réver accounted for the close relationship between raça e amor, however, I began to feel about the game the way that one of the giants of the Clube's history does, or so I let myself believe. "From the moment you love the Clube, you fight for it, fight for victories, fight for titles," he offered, before assuring me that the exact combination of loving and fighting that was required in this effort was "peculiar" to Atlético. This comment may sound something like the Clube's version of the party line, and it probably is. Yet to have watched "Captain America" lead the charge for his side from the back, chipping in with the not infrequent goal on occasion, for good measure, is to have observed a player who has always been able to strike a workable balance between loving and fighting on the one hand and, on the other, the "fun" and "dedication" that Réver says have allowed him to fulfill the dream of "millions" of Brazilian children "as a high-level athlete."[65] We may still be dealing in the murkier realm of feelings with this description, but Réver's thoughts on raça are a welcome reminder that none of the emotions he mentions "happens" in a vacuum.

Réver would surely know. When asked about the impact that COVID-19 had had on players at large, he spoke with great candor about such feelings as perhaps not every professional footballer would admit to having. "We've had a very difficult time these past two years," he said. "The uncertainty of the disease, the risks, the protocols. For me, playing without the support of the fans was the saddest point."[66] Not only that, but Réver went on to recall how, as he related to me, "the disease came and scared the world," superstar athletes included. This walking embodiment of raça, in other words, had the courage to talk about feelings that made him seem less than invulnerable. COVID-19, by his count, had brought sadness, fear, difficulty, and uncertainty to people everywhere, such that raça e amor may or may not have become an afterthought for them, at least for a time.

Looking back, I find it poignant that Réver should also have remarked on how "we've been out of [the] games for a while." He was referring to futebol matches in his own country, and how the return of the same "was positive for the mental health of Brazilians."[67] Some five weeks later, for Atlético's 2–3 home loss on August 7, 2022, against Athletico Paranaense, Réver himself had been named in the starting squad ahead of what was being billed as an important match, yet he withdrew from consideration after declaring that he was "emotionally unprepared" to play because of an illness in his family. Many such instances with a variety of players, in all countries, occurred during the COVID era. Réver's inability to play on the day in question is to this extent unremarkable, but it is another illustration of the fact that our emotionally charged feelings about football are no more containable than the game itself.[68]

3

Amor

> The only regret I will have in dying is if it is
> not for love.
>
> —GABRIEL GARCÍA MÁRQUEZ, *Love in the Time
> of Cholera* (1985)

What Sigmund Freud said about *futebol* bears repeating. The trouble is that the modern European father of psychoanalysis never makes explicit mention of sport in his once de rigueur writings on the mind, which are otherwise instructive for their insights into the human penchant for play. In such early works as *Jokes and Their Relation to the Unconscious* (1905) and *Creative Writers and Day-Dreaming* (1908), Freud posits that childhood is the stage in our development when we learn about play's potential for pleasure through rituals of what one observer names "psychical release."[1] Without ever designating any "ludic drive" as such, in the essay "Beyond the Pleasure Principle" (1920), Freud shifts his attention to the playful behaviors of adults, whose compulsion for repetition—a "death drive," Freud calls it—recent commentators have used to account for the untoward displays of aggression that typify competitive sports in the United States today.[2] What matters most in this abbreviated survey for our purposes is that Freud's initial interest in an "erotics" of love would eventually lead him to death as an explanation for the causes and effects of people's tendency to play. In other words, Freud wouldn't have needed a pandemic to appreciate a remark made by a character in Gabriel García Márquez's novel *Love in the Time of Cholera*

(1985), who says, "The only regret I will have in dying is if it is not for love."[3] For Freud, living, dying, loving, and playing flow from a common source of emotional expression that the faint-hearted sports fan would probably have a hard time fathoming. I met no such fans of Clube Atlético Mineiro (CAM). Their feelings about futebol ran deep under COVID-19, even though these quite plausibly could have proven fatal.[4]

We might well wonder how much love CAM's "players" were able to summon for their Clube in an age of contagion. Indeed, it's worth asking whether they've *ever* struck a healthy emotional balance between the loving and "fighting" that Atlético Mineiro's motto, *raça e amor*, proclaims even in the best of times. If we want to understand CAM, in other words, we need to consider the nature of the relationship between the two contradictory emotions that Atlético Mineiro claims as a badge of self-identification. For the process by which the "guts" of a professional footballer should be transformed into the feelings that we would normally associate with amor makes no more immediate sense than how the individualistic "desire" of the Brazilian footballer to defy destiny can be said to square with the demand that mascot Galo makes of every player to disregard his own needs for those of the team. All in all, loving Atlético Mineiro seems less complicated than the Clube's own relation to amor, especially if we subscribe to the "contagion theory" of crowd psychology that social scientists have advanced to account for the violence that historically has accompanied the emotional attachments of the most partisan football supporters in South America and Europe.[5]

No matter how much credence we give to *atleticanos* who claim to have the most passion, or *paixão*, of all club sides in the Brasileirão, we can allow that Galo has decidedly strong feelings about feelings. Director Helvécio Marins Jr. captures these feelings with dramatic effect in his 2021 film *Lutar, lutar, lutar*, which he codirected with Sérgio Borges. Taken from the lyrics of the anthem that Vicente Mota composed for CAM in 1969, the words from the title of Marins's film roughly translate into English as "Fight, Fight, Fight" or "Strive, Strive, Strive." This translation is appropriate, given that *Lutar, lutar, lutar* not only bids to tell CAM's emotional history but does so in the form of an embattled "love" story featuring fans who believe that despite Atlético's periods of storied glory, they must defend their Clube from being put upon by its bitter rivals.[6]

In his conversations with me, Marins laid bare the extent of his emotional involvement in his project: "It is hard with Galo to be strictly objective," he said.[7] And considering his upbringing, it is easy to see why he feels this way. Having grown up in comfortable circumstances within the vicinity of the Mineirão in the late 1970s and early 1980s, Marins was fortunate enough to be able to attend both of Atlético's weekly matches (with game days falling on Wednesdays and Sundays in that era) when these were played at home. His father, an engineer, spent much of the work week on the road, so he and his son attended the weekend fixtures together. Marins went to the midweek matches with Rogério, the Black handyman who lived in the guesthouse that was situated on the family's property in the Belo Horizonte neighborhood of Pampulha. Hard-working, hard-drinking, and knowledgeable about the game, Rogério died well before his time, in his thirties, from cirrhosis of the liver. Yet before his passing, he indoctrinated his young charge into a demotic sports culture that Marins would have me understand took on a different meaning from the populist vantage of the stands, where the future filmmaker learned to look, by his own telling, for a Black atleticano to embrace whenever CAM scored. "Galo took me out of my middle-class bubble," Marins reckoned, in the sense that he came to identify with the lives of the working-class people (many of them persons of color) who stood beside him in support of the Clube they all supported. Asked about the creative "play" of the artist that he is, Marins responded in a roundabout way to suggest that his struggles as a filmmaker (*Lutar, lutar, lutar* was eight years in the making) have continued to draw him closer to the life experiences of those whom he called "normal people," or "real Brazilian people," who "know what it means to suffer" and "struggle." "That's why I like Black people," he said. And that's why, as a supporter of Atlético Mineiro—which is to say, as someone who believes that he's "suffered" more than most—he identifies with the ethnic sections of a stadium where more or less everyone, Marins explained, "grows up with a feeling of injustice." Rather than allow this "feeling" to sour them, however, the Clube's supporters have come to equate it with a "love" that, Marins maintained, Atlético epitomizes. "It's about humanity," he said. "It's about life." He thus regards the "mixing" of the black-and-white stripes from CAM's official kits as a fitting symbol of the sentiments that sustain Galo's eight million fans, who, Marins averred, are prepared to "love, even when we don't win." And that's amor—or, that's amor according to a member of *A Massa* whose formative impressions of sport, instilled in him by a surrogate Freudian father of sorts, serve him in adulthood as the source of an aesthetic that the director said owes everything to the social psychology of "the people" for whom he carries a lasting affection.[8]

For Alice Quintão Soares, amor is colored by a politics even more forthright than Marins's vision of racial integration. "Alice," as she is known, is one of the founders of Grupa, a feminist collective whose members have united in their opposition to what she described (in impeccable English) as "sexism in soccer."[9] The group traces its origins to 2016, when several women supporters independently expressed their outrage on ESPN Brasil's fan blog over CAM's annual reveal of its new team jerseys. It was not that the women objected to the apparel's only being offered in men's sizes, a retail practice that would thereafter change. What prompted the soon-to-be organizers of Grupa to protest, rather, were the scantily clad female models who had been hired to sport CAM's kits while pacing the catwalk that had been prepared for the purpose. Offended by this display, "we decided to fight," Alice said. Before long, they were combatting other forms of prejudice as well, including the racism, homophobia, and misogyny that Alice regards as endemic to the game of football as it has been played in Brazil dating back decades. Grupa's outspokenness has brought it a fair share of media coverage, most notably by Globo TV, which airs many of CAM's matches. With this coverage has come a modicum of respect from Atlético Mineiro's administrators, "who take us seriously," Alice told me. Grupa's public exposure has also made it the target of online trolls on Twitter/X and Instagram. Many of these "commentators" have levied the same charge against the collective that I have made (without malice, I can assure you) against scholars whose overriding interest in sports seems to reside primarily in its capacity to serve them as a vehicle for making one or another form of political statement. Alice denied that she and the rest of the 120 current members of Grupa are "using the Clube like a political trampoline." Nor does she regard Grupa's mandate to "fight for inclusion," as she stated, to be inconsistent with the feelings she has as someone with strong emotional ties to CAM. Alice spoke for all Grupa members when she declared, "We love Galo. We are not here to fight Galo. We just want to help the Clube be better, more inclusive, more progressive." Alice assured me, "We *are* Galo," explaining that Grupa is "fighting" *for* the Clube, not against it.[10]

For all her politicking, Alice let me know that her love for the Clube could hardly be more personal or playful. Marins characterized his own connection to CAM as a kind of baptism into Blackness that has resulted from a process of what Eric Lott describes as "love and theft."[11] Alice, by contrast, recounted a family dynamic less Oedipal in its dramatic overtones than conventional, but that had been no less effective at orienting her emotions as an atleticana. As the daughter of a father without sons, Alice inherited the love her *pai* has for CAM and accordingly "grew up in the stadium," she told me, watching matches at the Mineirão with a man with whom her relationship continues to this day to revolve around Atlético Mineiro. In this respect, "I was a very lucky girl," Alice emphasized. Yet she also recognizes that, however much she might have been born into amor, "there is," she related, "a cultural thing [at Atlético Mineiro] that is bigger than football." Belo Horizonte's being, in Alice's description, "a provincial, conservative city" has meant that the isolated family structures that otherwise bleed new supporters into Galo are, in fact, inclusive of an entire Minas Gerais region that encourages an almost familial attachment to the footballers who represent the state's best-supported side. In Alice's eyes, Grupa is proof that sons as well as daughters are welcome in this extended family. Not only that, but she regards Grupa's staunch support for Clube Atlético Mineiro Feminino, the women's team that CAM sponsors as a precondition for its participation in the Copa Libertadores, as being of a piece with her feelings for the men's side. "Anything about Galo is Galo," she stated—and she meant it, despite the difficulties of attending matches for *Os Vingadores* (The Avengers), as the women's team is colloquially known, at out-of-the-way places and inconvenient times, such as mid-afternoon kickoffs on weekdays. Still, despite the many obstacles she's faced in expressing her sentiments for sport, Alice is sure that "it's harder to do Grupa than to do Galo." The former is unpaid labor, she reminded me, which she performs in the after-hours intervals away from a daytime job that had her working sixteen- to seventeen-hour shifts during the initial months of COVID-19. Those were dark days, Alice remembered, such that she was forced to take a six-month leave of absence from Grupa so that she could focus on her professional commitments in the public sector at a moment of societal crisis. But, much like the players who enter Atlético as employees and leave the Clube (if leave they must) as supporters—*Entra funcionário e sai torcedor* is the popular saying to this effect in Brazil—Alice reserves a place in her heart for an amor to which she's been bred.[12]

Other hearts have been corrupted by the game as it's played in Brazil. Even Atlético Mineiro has been tainted by futebol's sordid history of sexual violence and domestic abuse against women. CAM's record in this regard is no worse than that of other clubs inside the country. As Brenda Elsey and Joshua Nadel have shown, Brazil has long since policed women's participation in sports of every sort.[13] Until 1979, it prohibited women by law from playing futebol at all. My Clube, of course, likes to boast that it loves the most, which makes Atlético's failures to demonstrate a consistent level of respect for women feel egregious. This inconsistency is very much the case with the sometime Atlético player Robson de Souza, better known as "Robinho." Reared at the Brazilian club Santos in São Paulo, Robinho is remembered by many fans of the game today as an attacking player who showed flashes of great promise during his spells at established European heavyweights, including Real Madrid, Manchester City, and AC Milan. Yet Robinho's legacy is increasingly being rewritten in accordance with the part he played in the gang rape of a twenty-three-year-old Albanian woman at a nightclub in Milan, Italy, in November 2013. Convicted in absentia in 2017 for his participation in this crime, Robinho avoided extradition to Europe long enough to continue a playing career that subsequently took him to a number of other clubs, including Atlético Mineiro.[14] Signed by CAM in 2016 with much controversy, Robinho remained with Atlético until the completion of his contract in December 2017, ending a stay that Alice's Grupa had been vocal in protesting.[15]

Grupa was no more pleased by the return to CAM of former manager Cuca in 2021, after his initial spell with Atlético between 2011 and 2013. As a player in his own right for the Porto Alegre side Grêmio, Cuca, too, had been arrested for taking part in a gang rape, in his case involving a thirteen-year-old girl whom Cuca and three of his teammates encountered during their team's tour of Bern, Switzerland, in 1987. Held for thirty days at the time of the incident, Cuca and company were convicted two years later but never formally taken into custody to serve their respective prison sentences.[16] At the start of the current decade, the Brazilian Forum on Public Security indicated that 66,123 rapes had occurred in Brazil in 2020 alone, or one every eight minutes. Nearly 86 percent of the victims were female, and 60 percent of these victims were under the age of fourteen.[17] Thus, Grupa's #CucaNao campaign on Twitter in 2021 to register its members' opposition to CAM's reappointment of Cuca as coach was hardly an overreaction.[18] For a Clube that says it stands for amor, the rehiring of a reputed sex offender as its senior pitch-side representative is frankly inconsistent with the team's vaunted feelings, which a supporter of Atlético need not be a feminist to want to defend.

Marins let me know that "the players show us raça, and we love them for it."[19] Yet the circular nature of this assertion does nothing to explain what happens when the feelings of those who love a Clube like Atlético turn sour. André Martins to this end characterizes Argentine football as a "strongly self-referential discursive environment," where the players on the pitch and the "players" in the stands forge close emotional bonds that give rise to a kind of "collective personality."[20] But if the feelings that players share are the "negative emotions," or *emoções negativas*, that one recent observer of Brazilian futebol has characterized as a constituent element of the game, then play would appear to be productive of something other than the pleasure that long-suffering (or so they will tell you) supporters of Atlético inclusive of the constructive critics of Grupa know better than to take for granted.[21] Marins duly said that "raça comes from everything we suffered over the years." And with this observation, he pointedly referred to Atlético's outrageous Libertadores exit to Flamengo in a special playoff match arranged between the two sides in August 1981.[22] For Galo, the pain from this loss still smarts, but that's not to say that players who had yet to be born at the time of this historic setback can just lay claim to being included in the "we" that Marins mentions in his remembrance of what remains, in his mind, a catastrophe from which the Clube hasn't recovered. Nor can we know with any certainty whether the love that's often shown for Galo is fully reciprocated. CAM's longtime left winger Éder Aleixo spoke of "that display of love from the stands" at Atlético Mineiro's home matches without mentioning whether these feelings were mutual.[23] The dwindling attendance figures at all levels of state championship futebol in Minas Gerais would further indicate that local fans' passion for the game may have cooled during the past decade.[24] CAM's strong man defensive midfielder from the 1970s Toninho Cerezo, whom many consider among the best to play in the position of all time, didn't have to affirm that he returned "that feeling" shown to him by the Mineirão's fans during his playing days. With tears welling in his eyes, he had this to say of amor to Marins: "It fucks you up."[25] This reaction is not to imply that anyone who's been touched by amor winds up in need of therapy; love for this "club of resistance" also comprises what journalist Fred Melo Paiva calls "such a beautiful story."[26] The purpose of this chapter is to relay that story with all its attendant emotional contradictions.

Lovers, Fighters, Players

For Galo, playing means competing, to have a "go" at life by taking the game to one's opponents.[27] A favorite chant of the *torcida* captures this feeling best: *Vai pra cima deles, Galo!* (Go after them, Rooster!). Atlético's players, it should be said, are no less inclined than most footballers to resorting to extra-legal means to gain an advantage on the pitch, what Brazilians once called *truques*. Sometimes an actual fight, known in the 1930s as a *sururu*, ensues during a match, too, with fans spilling out onto the field to participate. All is fair in love and football, I suppose, and nothing so much demonstrates the close correspondence between loving, fighting, and playing in CAM's emotional universe as a matchday at the Mineirão. At these times, and in this place, the force of that Atlético feeling is everything.

Journalist Paiva knows more than most about that feeling. As someone who makes his living by thinking and writing about Galo for Belo Horizonte's main newspaper, Paiva attends daily to the epic mood swings that structure his friend Marins's film and that determine, both would agree, the everyday lives of anyone who is emotionally attached to the Clube. Like Marins, Paiva conceives of raça as a form of physical and psychological *work*. It is the Clube's equivalent of the manual and mental labor that people "without privileges," in the reporter's words, have grown accustomed to because of the subaltern positions they occupy in Brazilian society. They "have had to fight" simply to stay alive, Paiva assured me, and so have been conditioned by experience to resist fortunes that others might describe as unfair.[28] As much as Galo dwells on the hardships of the past, however, or what Paiva characterizes as "smoky memories" and "incurable pathologies," Team Rooster is mostly motivated in his estimation by love in the ever-present tense.[29] And this feeling, Paiva wanted to convey, is the key to understanding the relation between raça e amor. "You must fight for your love under any circumstances," he said. "You are driven by this love; it's very intense." With some poetic license, I interpret Paiva's explanation, in turn, to mean that much as the past is always turning into the present, Galo's willingness to fight defies any temporal horizon. It is a condition of immanence, in which feelings that have accumulated through what Paiva called "*uncommon* effort" over time are forever on the brink of finding release. And when they do, they take the form of the fiercest of affections.[30]

As for the origins of amor as an emotion, Paiva would have his Rooster and eat it too. In relating how he came to have the love

for his Clube that he claims was "inherent to me as a child," Atlético Mineiro's most important beat writer let me know that amor
was "instilled" in him as an infant while being breastfed by his
mother. "It's a very pure love," he said, and no wonder—at least
one student of the game has spoken of the seemingly "ancestral"
connection between men and the spherical shape of the ball itself,
a symbolic representation of maternity that gives rise to what another commentator calls the "ludic-oedipal impulse."[31] Paiva also
maintained that his love for CAM is "unconditional," so much
so that he compared it to the feelings of a *corno manso*, or meek
cuckhold, which is to say a husband who forgives his wife despite
knowing of her infidelities. Galo has never been unfaithful to Paiva.
Still, the unstable nature of the figures of language that Paiva used
to talk about amor—tracing, as he did, his childhood love for Atlético back in time in maternal terms, before switching to a sexual
metaphor involving adults to speak of his postadolescent feelings
for the Clube—betrays what our journalist has described elsewhere
as "a mental confusion composed of elements of great complexity
that form the human being throughout life."[32] Lucky for Paiva that
Atlético's players needn't undergo the same "catharsis" that he did
to appreciate the meaning of amor.[33] Their actions on the pitch
speak volumes about the outcomes, as opposed to the origins, of
their feelings. With respect to individual players, then, "everything
is done for this love," Paiva told me. Any Atlético player who has
been truly touched by amor "gives himself away, body and soul,"
he said. A collective expression of this feeling also appears whenever we find "eleven men running after the ball with unified purpose," which is how CAM's players fight for love, Paiva told me,
without acknowledging the darker historical reality that many of
the Clube's players over the years have additionally loved to fight.
Paiva did concede the danger of groupthink to a game in which "everything can be justified in support of one's club." He deemed the
outward signs that we would typically associate with this mind-set
"a great fascist manifestation," whereby the partisan of any given
side is prepared to die for what he or she blindly considers "my
people, my symbols, my shirt against all others." Paiva admitted
that his own love for Galo "is not rational," while underscoring

that he and the rest of Atlético's fans "are not causing harm to society." Rather, he likened their feelings to "a tribal mentality [that] is inherent to the human condition" and that, when kept (more or less) in check, qualifies as the most "amazing" of emotions.[34] That the feelings for Atlético to which he was acculturated by the age of five or six might differ in kind from those he imbibed from his mother in infancy is not something that seemed to bother Paiva. "Happy are those who have Galo in their hearts," said another of CAM's most prominent supporters, Frederico Bolivar.[35] Never mind that "happiness" is something that many of CAM's most loyal fans would say has eluded them.

Rodolfo Gropen spoke to me of his love for Atlético in quasi-religious terms. In fact, his origin story for amor is almost Edenic in its outlines, except that it unfolds in reverse. Rather than being born into Paradise only to lose it, the teller of this tale came into the garden of sport that the Clube occupies—and that the prominent Belo Horizonte tax attorney served in an administrative capacity for a full ten years, between 2009 and 2019—after passing through repeated trials that tested the mettle of him and his entire family. In conversation with me at his well-appointed law office in Belo Horizonte's downtown Savassi district, Gropen opened by stating that his paternal grandparents had fled their persecution as Jews in Stalin's Soviet Union to arrive as immigrants in Brazil.[36] If Gropen has, until recently, been the ultimate "insider" at CAM, his lineage is anything but that of the fortunate son. Neither of his parents attended university; neither professed a love for CAM while young, although his father converted from his *flamenguista* ways to become an atleticano after he witnessed the tears his eldest child Rodolfo shed when Flamengo "stole" the 1980 Brazilian Championship from Galo over the course of a two-legged final that saw CAM's marksman Reinaldo inexplicably dismissed with a red card after scoring his second goal in the decisive last match of the season. As Gropen remembered it, his father "hated" Flamengo after he saw the "suffering" this eventual loss caused his fifteen-year-old son.[37] Gropen marks the moment as a rite of passage for himself too: "I lost my 'virginity' in terms of believing in everything on this very important day," he has commented. In this statement, he was referring to the off-the-pitch factors that many observers assume must have led the Brazilian Football Confederation (CBF) to want to award the Brasileirão title to a team from Rio, the same city where the confederation had its headquarters, at a time of comparative political disquiet in the country.[38]

Whether or not we are ready to embrace this reading of the Clube's history, we can accept the object lesson Gropen's story affords us on the generational impact of sport. After graduating with a law degree from Universidade Federal de Minas Gerais (UFMG), the same school in Belo Horizonte where I spent four months teaching in 2022, Gropen practiced law and pursued further graduate study in São Paulo for the remainder of his twenties. His access to the Clube he loved was limited during this time, but his passion for CAM, his *"amor de paixão,"* as he described it, was undiminished. Married by his early thirties, Gropen thereafter tapped into a whole new reserve of feelings that he had not known existed before. When we spoke, Gropen explained that the intensity of what most of us would regard as a "passion" normally exhausts itself after six months or so. Love, by contrast, he understood to be an emotion that matures with age. The one feeling was ephemeral; the other burned less brightly but endured. Gropen remains married today, and he understands his feelings for Atlético to be "uncommon" precisely because they retain their white heat, as would not be the case, he maintained, in the typical long-term relationship. Thus, Atlético Mineiro has come to represent for him an exceptional emotional state. Gropen keeps his passion for the Clube, even as he enjoys what has become for him the love of a lifetime.

This relationship has experienced some complications, to be sure. The year 2008 was especially difficult for Gropen, not least in the aftermath of CAM's lopsided defeat to Cruzeiro in the league that year. Distraught by the loss in his own right, Gropen was even more pained by the response that his two sons, then ages ten and eight, had at the time. The elder took to kicking the walls of the family home; the younger was reduced to the tears that inevitably seem to be shed whenever Galo surprises, delights, or disappoints. Remembering the sacrifices that his own father had made to console Gropen after Atlético's loss to Flamengo in the 1980 Championship, our attorney took matters into hand after engaging in a lengthy discussion with a neighbor under the jaboticaba tree that stood in the yard of the latter's home. The upshot of this Adamic moment, at least in Gropen's own interpretation, is that he decided then and there to put himself forward for an administrative position at the Clube. Beginning in 2009, he served in three such roles. The first of these was a three-year term as managing director. That was followed by four more years of executive leadership as director of planning. Then came an additional three years as president of the board. Gropen stepped away from administration in 2019, receiving "not one penny," he assured me in timeless managerial speak, for this labor of love.[39] He has been compensated in other ways. Being *"atleticano doente"* (the pre-pandemic phrase translates as "sick" atleticano), as he called it, means that Gropen inhabits a "spiritual state" that he described as a kind of perpetual conversion experience. His amor is a love that doesn't lessen, much as raça means, in Gropen's own words, "not to know your limits, always going beyond." Winning or losing is not quite beside the point at Atlético, but it's also not even half the point. To say that someone is a "fanatic atleticano," then, is a "pleonasm," Gropen related, or a kind of verbal redundancy that applies more language than is necessary to explain what the term *raça e amor* should already make clear enough at face value. Atleticanos like to say that they have a profoundly emotional commitment to their Clube no matter what the state of play on the pitch. That commitment is encapsulated for them by a word, *amor*, or maybe two, *raça e amor*.[40]

Gropen applies this same extravagant standard to the players too. "The players themselves feel they have to give a little bit more than is possible," he told me. "We go beyond common limits for our passionate love." I asked Gropen how an executive at CAM could help promote this kind of culture at any football club, let alone CAM, and he attributed his own Clube's recent success in this regard to the leadership of the former Atlético president under whom he worked, Alexandre Kalil. More broadly, Gropen said that executives at Atlético are always looking for players "who will go beyond." Scouting the right variety of young talent is involved in this effort, as is coaching. Questions of team culture even arise during the negotiations involved in signing players. Gropen would surely know, given that he participated in the structuring of all the players' contracts during his time working at the Clube. Thus, we could say that CAM's culture of raça e amor is promoted at every level within the organization, from player recruitment and development through the legal negotiations over wages. Gropen was also keen to discuss how CAM "protects" its players, something he claimed that not all clubs in Brazil take the trouble to do. This kind of nurturing helps draw the Clube closer together, he said, further fostering the familial culture it wants to create. Indeed, the Clube is especially protective of "players without a crib," Gropen emphasized, meaning those who have not enjoyed the privileges of children raised in a "golden crib," or berço de ouro, as the saying in Brazil goes. Pertinent to this discussion, Gropen reminded me that many professional footballers come from poor families. Some of them also, he acknowledged, end up losing everything they earn, often due to the constant financial demands made on them by their extended families. Atlético Mineiro does what it can to assist players in avoiding these pitfalls of the professional game. CAM's youth team maintains on its staff social workers as well as child psychologists, for example, a policy that Freud no doubt would have applauded. If love is the "drug" that Gropen said that it is, then he and the rest of the atleticanos of the Clube's extended family would make no apologies for their addiction to something, or someone, that has sustained them in such good stead for so long. Nor do they offer any excuses for their enthrallment to feelings that resonate with the slogan that appears on the face of the Mineirão's stands: Nos somos o Atlético Mineiro (We are the Atlético Mineiro). CAM may be the club that fights, but, for Gropen, it is also the club that cares.[41]

I learned the hard way how much Atlético can hurt a person's feelings, during the second leg of its round of 16 matches against Flamengo in the 2022 edition of the Copa do Brasil. CAM had won the home meeting in the tie at the end of June, looking comfortable up 2–0 before conceding a late goal to the visitors. In the reverse fixture in front of some seventy thousand fans at the Maracanã on Wednesday, July 13, Atlético was never really in the match. Not only had the tables been turned; the playing field seemed tilted, as if the home side were running downhill at Galo for the full ninety minutes of a game played in a light winter's rain. Atlético showed effort, but not its usual zealousness. The team expended itself physically, but without the invention and emotion that supporters say sets CAM apart from the rest of the pack. Atlético's *voz da torcida*, its "voice of the supporters," Carol Leandro, took notice after the 2–0 defeat, telling the Globo TV podcast in which she stars, "Galo didn't play at all!"[42] Gropen concurred, admitting what no member of A Massa likes to concede: The Flamengo team was clearly more *raçudo* on the night. Gropen was philosophical about the loss, repeating the small consolation offered by what he called "soccer jargon" by telling me, "*Bola pra frente*" (We move on).[43] And indeed, CAM did begin to redirect its attention to other upcoming encounters, just not in this competition. A writer for Globo.com reckoned the loss in monetary terms, reporting that while the Clube may have earned R$4.9 million (approximately US$925,655) in reaching this stage of the Copa, it would miss out on the additional R$3.9 million (approximately US$736,745) it could have earned by advancing to the quarterfinals.[44] For my part, I didn't doubt the math involved in these calculations, but I did sense that the human interest in this story resided elsewhere, in the *emotional* angles of a sport whose fans will remind you that theirs is "more than a game."[45]

As dejected as she was by Atlético's setback in the Copa, Leandro suggested to me a different way of thinking about these feelings, one that has served her well in her role as a spokesperson for Galo's supporters. "I have always loved Galo," Leandro told me when we talked in late July 2022.[46] She even admitted to having done "stupid things" for this love as a teenager, such as skipping classes at school for a semester so she could work to earn enough money to attend matches. Now that she carries what she called the "immense responsibility" of representing A Massa, however—GaloTV hired Leandro in March 2022, on the strength of the reputation she made narrating *Lutar, lutar, lutar*—she approaches these affairs of the heart with what seems to be a seasoned maturity. Like the rest of the people with whom I spoke, she described her amor as indivisible from the raça she agreed defies translation.[47] Her outlook on love sounded familiar in this respect, as did her view that amor is all about "going beyond the limits" of what is logical and plausible, much as the supporters at Atlético "love" the players "who go beyond, who make every effort" on the field of play. These conventional (by CAM's standards) attitudes notwithstanding, Leandro also told me that "unconditional love is something that doesn't exist" because "Galo isn't tangible." Leandro explained that she can come face to face with her mother and say that she loves her, for example, but that urging Atlético on at matches is, by comparison, like "screaming to the emptiness of the sky."[48] Thus, not only does Leandro regard CAM's iconic shield as little more than an imaginary placeholder for Galo, the Rooster itself being, in the ironic estimation of this paid proxy for A Massa, a mere *representation* of an associative ideal (Figure 3.1); she looks upon both as free-floating signifiers of sorts, faint gestures in the direction of feelings they can never actually embody.[49] "We have this feeling that we can't live without Galo," Leandro continued. "But rationally," she said, "we know we *can* live without Galo, even though we will never stop dedicating ourselves to Galo."[50] Leandro's thoughts on amor finally amounted to something other than the ordinary sports metaphor. Not only does she feel strongly enough about Atlético to have fallen head over heels in love with a representative *sign* of her affections; she has the self-awareness to admit that she doesn't require a "real" Rooster to validate the feelings she has for the Clube.

I was still working through the permutations of amor the morning after I spoke with Leandro, when I visited Márcio de Lima Leite at the Casa Fiat de Cultura. *A voz da torcida* had told me, in her own words, "My story with Galo starts upside down," by which she meant that her love for Atlético had not been passed down to her from within her family, as is frequently the case in Minas Gerais. Her father, in fact, was *cruzeirense*, a supporter of CAM's rival Cruzeiro Esporte Clube, and tried his best to convince his daughter to bleed the blue of that unmentionable crosstown side he supported.[51] Leite has met with no such resistance in expressing his first and lasting love for CAM, yet his understanding of amor is no less a study in indirection than Leandro's. Speaking

Figure 3.1 Clube Atlético Mineiro's shield, in the team's signature black and white. (*Courtesy Clube Atlético Mineiro.*)

from the modernist-inspired arts and culture center that the previously named multinational car manufacturer maintains beside Belo Horizonte's central Praça da Liberdade, Leite (who doesn't really like football) told me that he had only "two loves" in life outside his family: Elvis Presley and CAM.[52] His wife, son, and daughter are similarly atleticano and every day indulge Leite's enthusiasms in conversation. But no matter how "balanced" Leite's love for his family might be, the love he feels for Galo represents the exception to the rule of his customary equanimity. This observation is not to suggest that Leite, who was installed in May 2022 as the president of Brazil's Associação Nacional dos Fabricantes de Veículos Automotores (Association of Automotive Vehicle Manufacturers [ANFAVEA]), and who additionally serves as the legal and institutional director of the Stellantis automotive group for all South America, has been unhinged by the emotions he has for CAM. Rather, he gives in to his feelings for Galo with the knowledge that he will never entirely reconcile a head for business and a heart that may, on occasion, skip a beat whenever he passes by the Clube's headquarters in Lourdes, where he also sits on CAM's board. We might say that Leite's amor is compounded of sense and sensibility, with the emotional portion of this mixture just getting the better of our respected corporate executive's conditioned appreciation for the bottom line.[53]

To anyone who would say that love and money don't mix inside what scholars call "the working ecosystem of Brazilian football," Leite is quick to point out that futebol has played an important part in forming the more than twenty thousand employees at Stellantis (many of them Atlético supporters) into a "family."[54] Stellantis had yet to establish a formal relationship with CAM at the time of my writing, due in part to several sticking points that the corporation wanted to address before making any long-term commitment to the Belo Horizonte sports organization. First, issues of financial compliance need to be considered. Stellantis would hesitate to associate itself with any club, including CAM, that ran afoul of such regulations as the Brazilian government has put in place to prevent financial improprieties being tolerated at the professional levels of the country's football establishment. Questions of "diversity and inclusion" also demand attention. "At Stellantis, we cannot accept discrimination," Leite informed me. "We have a conduct code." And so, no matter how much Atlético's supporters might delight in the lyrics to traditional songs like "Maria, I know you tremble," the rollicking queer-baiting number that the *torcida* reserves for its special foe, Cruzeiro, Leite knows that the principles for which Stellantis stands require that the Clube forego promoting an atavistic version of its own identity at the expense of others. Leite was accordingly engaged in discussions with CAM's president, Sérgio Coelho, to find ways to "transform" the culture at Atlético so the two sides they represent could negotiate a sponsorship deal that would serve the purposes of both parties.[55]

If Leite brings a relative progressivism to the bargaining table, his mindfulness for what he calls "image" makes his love for the Clube not unlike Leandro's, which she allows is an agreed-upon fiction. Leandro cares a great deal for Galo but remains acutely conscious of loving a something that might be a nothing. Leite, meanwhile, was being candid about the optics of corporate politics when he admitted that there are certain constraints upon the feelings he can show for his Clube in public. This statement is not to suggest that his emotions aren't genuine—to hear Leite recite one or another of the chants from CAM's unofficial songbook is to know that his open avowals of support for Atlético are more than a canny performance for the would-be buyers of Fiat's automobiles.[56] Still, none of the "love" the players in this chapter have expressed carries all the poetic connotations that we might expect from the word *amor*. Shadowed by the specter of the pandemic on the one hand, clouded by the almighty sign of the Brazilian currency, the *real*, on the other, the feelings that Atlético's lovers hold for their Clube appeared to me to circulate as closely to the common marketplace as they did to the morgue. The one love was wholly negotiable; the other was anything but.

More or Less Amor

As the president of Atlético Mineiro from 1926 to 1930, Leandro Castilho de Moura Costa became an icon of the Clube he loved. A brief biographical sketch of him that appeared in the "Esportes" section of *Jornal Estado de Minas* in April 1950 remembers the lawyer and forward-thinking administrator as having given his "body and soul" to the team that thrived under his tenure. "For him, Atlético was his life," the paper reports, despite the president's being unable to cope with the emotions that he experienced while attending Galo's matches in person.[57] Costa often spent much of his time during home games outside the team's brand-new stadium in Lourdes, asking passersby for match updates as he paced the streets along blocks of a once-vacant area of Belo Horizonte. It was under Costa's watch (figuratively speaking) that Atlético won the Minas Gerais league championship of 1926–27, with the *Trio Maldito* (Unholy Trio) of potent attacking players that the president had helped assemble—Jairo, Said, and Mário de Castro—doing its part to end América-MG's run of dominance in the state. We could say that Costa's love for Atlético burned brightly, as evidenced by his decision to bring electric power to a stadium in Lourdes that, after lighting up on August 9, 1930, became a source of modernizing pride for people throughout the Minas region. This is what love looked like to one atleticano who looms large in the Clube's history.[58]

My own feelings for futebol are such that I continued to travel to the Mineirão to watch Atlético's matches live on occasion while I remained in Belo Horizonte. One such visit occurred in the early evening of Sunday, July 24, 2022, when Atlético squared off against the São Paulo side Corinthians. The latter was not a team to be taken lightly. Much as my Clube does in "BH" (Belo Horizonte's initials are pronounced "beh-ah-GAH" in the local dialect), Corinthians claims the mantle as the people's club of its respective city, the largest in the Southern Hemisphere. It was also sitting second in the Brasileirão table when it rolled into town, with Atlético looking little more than average as of late. The defensive frailties that had weakened the team for months were still a liability. With thirty games to go in the season, moreover, the Clube was short on ideas going forward. Atlético's board was worried enough by the team's state of play to show manager Antonio Mohamed the door after the midweek draw against Cuiabá, with the aforementioned Cuca being named as his replacement (Cuca had stepped away from the Clube for personal reasons after the title-winning season of 2021) the day before the match with Corinthians. Asked in early July about the reputed interest shown in his managerial services by the Buenos Aires side Boca Juniors, Cuca had told the Argentine press, "This year I don't work."[59] Turk or no Turk—and the unseemliness of the controversial Cuca's return notwithstanding—I was in the stands with the rest of the afflicted to watch my team get a win.

COVID-19 numbers had been climbing at that period in Belo Horizonte, as they were across much of the United States. Not to get political, but my own brother, Jonathan, seemingly immune to the disease that almost took our mother from us, tested positive for the coronavirus in Austin, Texas, the same day as U.S. president Joe Biden. Back at the Mineirão, I saw a few more masked spectators than I had at the match that I attended in June, but this shift represented no real improvement, since the fifty-six thousand people who turned out for the game in July were more than double the number counted at the earlier contest. Galo was feeling itself, regardless. I arrived extra early for the match against Corinthians, and I was wise to do so. Seated as I was in the heart of the torcida, rubbing shoulders with the supporters' groups in the *laranja inferior* section of the stadium near the corner behind the away team's goal, I found myself surrounded by an A Massa that was undeterred by Atlético's middling form. Seats were few. Elbowroom was limited. And the *cerveja* flowed freely, the *mineiros* being a beer-drinking people. There was also the unmistakable trace of reefer in the air, the Rooster apparently having a fondness for that medicinal weed. But what stood out to me most on the day of this midwinter 6:00 P.M. kickoff was the current of passion that ran through the crowd. The occasional cannon fire heard in the stadium drew the resounding, well-drilled response, "GALO." Songs were sung. Arms were raised and waved in unison. And the home team's emergence onto the pitch was met with a roar that rocked the Mineirão's foundations. These observations are more than sports clichés—I was there. I felt these things in common with the rest of the crazies who were keeping me company inside what seemed more a "dramatic happening" than a prearranged spectacle.[60]

Galo came. Galo saw. Galo lost to a Corinthians side that, frankly, seemed to be the better outfit. As the team is wont to do when I watch a match in person, we scored first, in this case after a neat looping shot in the ninth minute to the right of the away team's goal. This goal came courtesy of Keno, Atlético's left-winger on the night and a player who is only ever up for a fight. Celebrations ensued for a few minutes afterward. Among the highlights of these was the fair amount of beer (I don't drink) cascading down from the sections of seats above us, but it would have taken more than this shower to drench my spirits, for what followed this opening action was more Galo, and then more Galo. My Clube peppered the opponent's goal with a succession of shots, none of them making their way past a busy Corinthians goalkeeper. Our opponents, for their part, were never given a real opportunity to play. Atlético Mineiro snuffed them out each time the away side ventured forward, and this pattern held until about fifteen minutes into the second half. At around the seventieth minute, however, Atlético did not so much retreat as they decided, almost to a man, to stand back a bit from the opposition. They didn't quit, yet they were no longer the aggressors. Finally allowed to play, Corinthians did just that, scoring an eightieth-minute equalizer before taking the lead after being awarded a penalty kick just six minutes later. A healthy dose of stoppage time afforded the home team no real chance to score again on the night. Those who stayed to the very end of the match—and most did—serenaded the players regardless. In any other context, the lyrics to their songs might have seemed more a form of madness than amor. Atlético's anthem announces in its opening stanza that its supporters "vibrate" (*vibramos*) to the team's victories. But even in defeat, "we" play with much raça e amor (*Jogamos com muita raça e amor*). Not only that, but atleticanos pledge to keep playing until they die, as their anthem's refrain repeats no fewer than four times with the line "*Uma vez até morrer!*" Love and death, indeed.

The Clube's organized fan base leads the line for Atlético in taking what is something of a fundamentalist position in the expression of these feelings. A 2017 study showed that 13.4 percent of CAM's supporters belong to the *torcidas organizadas* that make such a demonstrative display of their emotions at matches, as they did in the game with Corinthians that I attended. That percentage might not sound like much, but the members of the torcida more than make up for their comparative lack of numbers with an ardor that literally shakes stadiums. Most of these organized supporters are single and male, with a median age of roughly twenty-eight years. They love their Clube without reservation. And not only are they found to be receptive to leisure activities in general—some 26 percent of CAM's organized support comes from students, who may well be predisposed to play—they take their support for their Clube most seriously, as can be seen when they continue to turn out for CAM during those less than successful seasons that the more casual fan would like to forget.[61]

The successful patch in which the Clube found itself at the time of my writing should not disguise the fact that it has made a historical habit of finishing runners-up to the winners of any number of titles to which Galo only pretended in the end. We already know about the fifty-year wait between the Clube's two triumphs in the Brasileirão in 1971 and 2021. The loss to Flamengo in the league championship of 1980 is likewise legendary, as is the team's exit to the same team in the Copa Libertadores of 1981. This is not even to mention Atlético's succumbing to São Paulo FC in the Brasileirão that was contested (in every sense of the word) in 1977. Despite the military's tampering that year with the structure of the league, which saw the first division of Brazilian football swell to an impracticable sixty-two teams, Atlético Mineiro finished the regular season undefeated and ten points clear of São Paulo, yet it was somehow still required to face that same side in a playoff final that went to penalties. It goes without saying that the result went against the *alvinegro*, and atleticanos to this day hold a grudge stemming from this loss alongside the love and the "fight" they carry as part of their enthrallment to the Clube. Inured to the worst of having its feelings hurt, Galo neither expects nor seeks any special dispensation for the heartache it's endured over the years; none of the supporters with whom I spoke wanted my sympathy, at any rate. This feeling held true for the civilian supporters of my acquaintance and for the diehard members of the torcida. And, of course, anyone who joined in the singing of CAM's anthem was making an emotional commitment that registered his or her readiness to die (*morrer*) for the Clube. The supporters I met expressed this last sentiment with more pride than regret.

That I should willingly occupy my place within this lethal sporting environment returns us to a question that I broached earlier: Does my support for Atlético Mineiro qualify as a conscious "choice"? It certainly amounts to a peculiar form of play, whatever else we might say about the causal factors behind my affective attachments as a football-addled adult. In fact, so long as we are interrogating my motives, we might also ask why an American English professor should be looking for love way down south in Minas Gerais in the first place. Some would probably be inclined to say that I represent the worst kind of global tourist, using the privileges of my U.S. passport to search the world over for such pleasures as a favorable exchange rate allows me to pay. Or, if we prefer to keep things a little less personal, we could also ponder the broader cultural question posed by the Brazilian historian Hilário Franco Júnior, who writes, "Who can know Brazil better, on all levels, if not Brazilians?"[62] Grupa's Alice let me know that the Clube receives the love of supporters from all over the world with its far-flung "consulates," or *consulados do Galo*, located in cities throughout Brazil as well as such countries as Norway, Portugal, and the United States.[63] My love for the Clube was thus no anomaly. Franco Júnior nevertheless recognizes that the Brazilian who would study something as central to the country's self-image as futebol is subject to an "emotional involvement" that precludes him from thinking and writing objectively about a topic so close to his heart.[64] This same stipulation might also have applied to me. Then again, maybe an American for once had the better of the Brazilian when it came to the "serious" treatment of futebol. I can say that I believe that I have earned the right to pursue my work on play.

Straight from the Heart

Speaking in a television interview in the mid-1980s, Brazilian footballer Dario José dos Santos remarked, "Everything done with love succeeds. I always played football with love."[65] "Dario," as he is known, or "Dadá Maravilha" (Wonder Dadá), would offer this opinion, of which he had many, toward the end of a twenty-year playing career that saw him play for seventeen different clubs. Dario played for CAM on three different occasions, first from 1968 to 1972, then again in 1974, and for a final time during the 1978–79 season. The last of these campaigns was not as successful as Dario's previous spells with the Clube, yet atleticanos will never forget that he scored the only goal in the final match of the 1971 season—a trademark header, against opponents Botafogo—clinching the first of Atlético's Campeonato Brasileiro titles. Some forty-six years later, a reporter referred to Dadá Maravilha as one of the best-known *ciganos* (gypsies) of domestic football.[66] The implication was that whatever love the player felt for his serial employers, Dario was forever in search of his next professional contract.[67] This fact is not to discount the feelings of a player whose stores of amor appear to have been at least as great as those of his peers. Dario did not remain in one place for very long, it's true, but he stayed in the game itself far longer than is typical for a player of his or any other era. In his above comments, Dadá equated love with "success." He could have related it to staying power as well. His butterfly tendencies notwithstanding, Dario stands out as someone who played the long game *because* of love . . .

. . . And money. A newspaper profile of Dadá Maravilha that ran in *Jornal dos Sports* back in 1979 features not only "proverbs" from a player who regaled the Brazilian press for years with his choice one-liners but also a kind of résumé of the different jobs he'd held before and after entering football professionally. Dario grew up poor as a boy in Rio de Janeiro. Of this formative period, he relates, "I wasn't into football. I just liked to run around the streets, with the kids. I jumped over the wall to steal mangos, and the dogs would attack me."[68] His obvious speed carried Dario out of those petty larcenous predicaments into the more promising positions he held as a paid manual laborer. Dario worked at first for a local electric company, digging and installing the posts for power lines; later, he switched to working for a beer company, performing the heavy lifting of delivery prior to serving as an office assistant for a firm that just so happened to have its own football team. Invited by his then-manager to participate, Dadá did not make much of an impression. Undeterred, he came to realize that he had found his true calling and from there would join the youth development squad at the modest club Campo Grande in his home city. Then came Atlético, where Dario made the name for himself that Brazilians of all sporting persuasions still recognize today.

Leavening his column with a few specimen samples of the gospel according to Dadá—"In life, wanting is power" and "For every problem, a solution" can stand in for the rest—the writer of *Jornal*'s miniature history of Dario's laboring life might be forgiven for composing what seems to be a self-help primer for a football-loving people. As the subject of this proverb-laden parable, Dario himself does more than enough to disabuse readers of the notion that his attitudes toward play might be misconstrued as political. They are not; they're profitable, as Dario underscores by saying, almost as an aside, "If Arena or MDB will give my children milk."[69] The remark comes in response to the reporter of this piece gently alluding to the player's habit of frequent leave-taking. What Dadá suggests with his reply, in turn, is that neither of the parties that featured in what at the time was Brazil's two-party political system, the incumbent military-backed National Renewal Alliance Party (ARENA) and the opposition MDB, which included nearly all contingents of the country's Labour Party as well as its Social Democrats, was likely to receive his love unless it also paid his wages. This comment did not make Dario a mercenary any more than a similar set of attitudes would some other player. But it did represent a stark admission that amor could be amortized over the term of a work contract, such that a player earned his keep at a club by apportioning out his love in installments of emotionally committed performances.

To say that Dadá Maravilha is in touch with the financial side of his feelings is not to accuse him of violating a shibboleth of the Clube that he by all appearances loved. Amor as it has been presented in these pages is no immaculate emotion, and Dario has long since shown that he had the character to play for a team that was a study in contrasts. Indeed, Dario is the player who would claim in 1984, "I'm still a thirty-eight-year-old boy."[70] As for Dadá's raça, he earned the additional nickname *Dario Peito de Aço* (Steel-Chested Dario) for reasons that he likes to put into his own words. In the same year that Dario informed the world of his endless love for futebol, for example, he told journalists that he didn't really know how to play the game, only how to score goals.[71] He tallied 113 of them during his career, and he was not particular about how these crossed the goal line, either. "There's no such thing as an ugly goal" is one of his memorable sayings. "What's ugly is not scoring."[72] Not known for his humility, moreover, Dario surmised his own greatness when he proclaimed, "There are three powers on Earth: God in Heaven, the Pope in the Vatican, and Dadá in the penalty area."[73] Or, in regard to the remarkable hang-time he displayed with his prowess for heading the ball, he offered this self-admiring description: "There are only three things that stop in the air: hummingbirds, helicopters, and Dadá Maravilha."[74] Aware of his human frailties, however, Dario also knew that his hyperbolic talk about his talents was meaningless unless it translated into performances out on the pitch. While nursing an injury in 1974, he thus made this public gut-check before rejoining CAM: "I know that to regain a place in the team I will have to fight hard."[75] Most would agree that the Brasileirão was better off with a player of Dario's abilities, along with the playful Dadá-isms that still resonate today. What Atlético the club lost without Dario in the side was a player who was unafraid to confront the contradictions of his own emotions, especially as these pertained to feelings that were no less heartfelt for being fungible.

Paulo Roberto Prestes has been similarly adept at finessing the emotional complexities that come from his longtime association with CAM. "Paulo Roberto," as he is known throughout Brazil, is a rare member of Atlético's elite five hundred club. He made 504 appearances for the team during his eleven years there as the side's starting left back, between 1986 and 1996. The player additionally captained the Clube for eight of those years, the result not only of his superior technique and tactical nous on the field but also what he described as his dependable displays of "responsibility and professionalism."[76]

These latter traits are not to be confused with raça, Paulo Roberto told me when we met at a café adjacent to Belo Horizonte's Praça da Liberdade on a late afternoon in early August that saw the city receive its first rainfall in two and a half months. Captaining the side was about doing one's job, he explained. Indeed, it sometimes entailed doing the coach's job, too, in an age when it was not the norm, as it is now, for teams to carry a technical staff of anywhere from eight to ten members. The role of the team's captain was therefore much more "evident" in those days, Paulo Roberto said. The manager, for instance, would often speak to him about the strengths and weaknesses of the team, and he, in turn, would sometimes take it upon himself to call for tactical changes on the pitch during matches. And when his teammates needed upbraiding on the field of play, Paulo Roberto would take care of that as well, even if, in his own words, he believed that "showing players how not to give up on a play" was possible only up to a point. He compared raça (what we were talking about) to a kind of "hunger." Having raça was about *not* having it; it required that a player supply something that was otherwise lacking and so convert a negative into a positive. Paulo Roberto maintained that players are usually "born with" raça, while suggesting that it can be cultivated to a certain extent under the right conditions.[77]

He viewed amor differently: "You can teach raça but not amor."[78] By way of demonstration, he invoked the *Lei Pelé* of 1998. Much of the formative work behind the so-called Pelé Law or Free Pass Law can be attributed to Hélio Viana de Freitas, who at the time was serving under the eponymous sporting legend as the vice president of the Deliberative Council of the National Institute for the Development of Sport. The purpose of the legislation in question was to bring greater transparency to the game of futebol in Brazil, namely by changing a "pass" (*o passe*) system that attached players to clubs beyond their employment contracts. Even when a contract expired within this old arrangement, a player was still bound to the club that held his *passe* until it granted him authorization to leave, prompting not a few players to resist what they felt was a kind of enslavement. In Paulo Roberto's day, players were considered free and clear of their "passes" after turning thirty-two years of age, but that was little compensation when so few of them were able to reach that advanced stage in careers that were typically short-lived. Paulo Roberto himself had six more months remaining on his contract with CAM when he reached his thirty-second birthday. He could still count on being the side's starting left back, his senior status notwithstanding. Yet like the rest of his teammates, he chafed at working for an employer that could be as much as three or four months late in paying players' wages, such was the state of the Clube's finances in that period. When Porto Alegre's Internacional came calling, then, offering Paulo Roberto the chance to finish his career where he'd started it, he believed that he had only one option. He cried.[79]

Paulo Roberto conceded that his wish to move (which the Clube granted) came down solely to money at a time when the sums that players earned had not yet reached the exponential figures they would in later decades. He nevertheless looks upon the replacement of the *passe* system as having been good and bad for a game that produces all too few Dadá Maravilhas. Rare is the player today who is contractually unbound but emotionally committed. Of course, players now enjoy higher wages and greater freedoms than they did before. But by becoming "entrepreneurs," which is how Paulo Roberto regards footballers these days, they have also denied themselves the emotional benefits, he said, that come from playing much or most of one's career with a single club. Our captain's point is that it is difficult under these circumstances for players to love their clubs or for clubs to even know their players. Thus, what Paulo Roberto described as the emotional "coldness" and "distance" that settled upon the game during the one-and-a-half years when supporters' attendance at matches was either forbidden or strictly limited by COVID-19 might not be as out of the ordinary as we think that they are. Paulo Roberto himself has stayed in the game by working as a radio and television broadcaster for CAM's matches, every one of which he watches with feelings that exceed even those he experienced as a player. And, like the players down on the pitch, he feeds off the "heat" of the supporters whose love makes all the difference, he's sure, between playing for CAM and playing for any other team in the league. Paulo Roberto knows what it means *vestir a camisa* (to wear the shirt). In his era, "players *wore* their jerseys," he told me. Their emotions were woven into the very fabric of the uniforms they wore on their well-conditioned backs. For these reasons, he considers his "passion" for CAM to be "like a second skin," he stated. "I'm a mineiro," Paulo Roberto continued, looking me straight in the eyes. "I'm going to be buried here"—a slave to love, it would seem.[80]

Among the former players who agreed to talk with me, several mentioned that I probably shouldn't even bother asking CAM's current squad about amor. Like Paulo Roberto, they had come to the realization that they could better appreciate the game they once played with distinction now that they no longer occupied a place between the lines. The suggestion was not that today's athletes are unfeeling automatons, going through the motions of playing without any emotions whatsoever. Rather, what Paulo Roberto and others recognized were the benefits of hindsight, which allowed them to see just how much the practical demands of matches had inhibited them from feeling amor in the moment.

It was comforting to know, I suppose, that amor ripened with age for those players who were prepared to wait for it. Dadá Maravilha might say that it increased with interest over time. But, like his friend Paulo Roberto, CAM's former defensive midfielder Heleno Oliveira described the love he associated with the Clube as something that was difficult to grasp. In his telling, amor "is stronger than simple affection." It's all-consuming, such that in his own case, his love for Atlético Mineiro afforded him a "life education" that "molded [his] personality."[81] I asked Oliveira what he had learned over the course of his 379 appearances for CAM between 1971 and 1985, during which time he helped the side pick up its first-ever league championship. These life lessons were "based on more than sport," he replied. They'd shown him that playing is about *other* people's wants and needs, or, in his own words, that "amor is about the supporters," whom Oliveira admiringly characterized as "nuts."[82] His feelings in this regard were informed by the extended time he'd served at the Clube, given that Oliveira entered CAM's academy at the age of thirteen and so had grown up within the culture of Atlético Mineiro in a way that is no longer the norm at CAM or any other professional sports organization. Oliveira regrets this change, saying that players today "can lose touch with what it means to be a supporter," which in turn makes it "very hard" for them "to have a *love* relationship with the Clube." Preoccupied as they allegedly are with what Oliveira called "branding" and "image," they have traded a "passion" that I interpret as a condition of emotional proximity for the cold distance that is dollars.[83] The supporters, meanwhile, continue to exchange their hard-earned *reais* for tickets to attend the Clube's matches, where they watch players who may or not be *feeling* it.

This circumstance doesn't mean that the players are incapable of reconciling futebol, feelings, and finance. Indeed, Rafael Miranda reminded me that players have always run great emotional risks by virtue of their participation in a game that is neither wholly a profession nor a pastime. Thus, keeping one's emotional distance from the Clube could be seen as a kind of defense mechanism, of avoiding the fire lest a person get burned by what Miranda called the "warmth" and "heat" of the game pre-COVID.[84] Miranda himself believed his responsibilities at Atlético Mineiro were a great "weight" when he played there, he said, and he would have gladly traded these responsibilities for the "pleasurable feelings" of the supporter he remains.[85] We've seen that great pain often accompanies these same supporters' pleasures, which doesn't necessarily invalidate Miranda's claim; his complex point is, in fact, well-taken. What Miranda was saying, I believe, is that pleasure itself is about "play," while playing the game of futebol (or any other risky business, from financial management to family life to freelance writing) is about a professionalism that often takes precedence for players over the feelings they experience while they're "at work." The risk that runs in the opposite direction is, of course, part of the argument on which this book rests. In short, the passion we have for play differentiates it from any of the other forms of work that we might otherwise look upon as a burden. Once we lose that loving feeling, once professionalism—or politics—puts play in what most adults have determined to be its subordinate place, then all we're left with is work and nothing but work.

As a writer, I like to believe that we don't have to put paid to playfulness simply because we've lost touch with the feelings that draw so many of us to sports in the first place. Maybe that's just wishful thinking. Or maybe, as I learned through an extended stay in one of Latin America's many football-mad nations, our irrational drive to keep playing, despite all the reasons we have not to, is what keeps us alive even during times of crisis, such as COVID-19. The current crop of players at CAM have had every financial reason to continue to suit up under conditions that were anything but conducive to play. To have seen the spring in their collective steps when they take to the pitch on matchdays, however, is to be confronted with a resiliency and spiritedness that suggest the propriety, the necessity, of play at times like these.

4

Post-match

> There was, once in a while, joy.
>
> —João Guimarães Rosa, "As margens
> da alegria" (1962)[1]

As the number of days remaining in my stay in Brazil ran down, I couldn't help but reflect on the general state of happiness, or *felicidade*, that my residence in Belo Horizonte had brought me. Nor, as someone who was writing a book about play, could I resist drawing a comparison between the *felicidade* I was feeling and the specific form of joy that Brazilians often (but by no means exclusively) associate with *futebol*, what they call *alegria*. I'd been happy in Brazil, and I was sad to be leaving. But I was also worried about my friends and colleagues there. For while I'd spent my time in Minas Gerais working through the finer points of sport and play, my acquaintances inside the country had been gripped by the approach of Brazil's upcoming presidential election on October 2, 2022, which pitted the then-incumbent conservative Jair Bolsonaro against his sometime predecessor, the Workers' Party candidate Luiz Inácio Lula da Silva, better known as "Lula." It was a winner-take-all contest that threatened to deepen Brazil's political divisions, and I cannot deny that I was glad that the date of my departure preceded what was sure to be an anxious affair. Then again, it might seem fitting that the author of a book that affords *play* a pride of place that's normally enjoyed by politics should be fleeing the scene of what proved to be a period of great disquiet in Brazil. Yet I must stress that it has never been my intention to allow my playful approach to *That Futebol Feeling* to substitute for a method of writing that's intellectually honest and ethically engaged. I simply want to change the way we think and talk and write about sport.

My sport of choice is futebol and, with it, all the emotions we associate with the game in a part of the world where the relationship between politics and sport is perhaps even more self-evident than it is in the United States. Witness the aftermath of Bolsonaro's eventual October 30 defeat to Lula in a special Sunday runoff election that saw thousands of Brazilians take to the streets of the country's largest cities. Bolsonaro, we know, alleged without any evidence in support of his claims that the election he'd lost after two separate rounds of balloting (the first round at the start of the month had been inconclusive) was marred by fraud. After Bolsonaro refused to concede, his supporters duly began blockading roads and highways throughout their large nation in protest of the election's outcome once results were known. It wasn't Brazil's politicians or even the police who settled matters in the short term; indeed, many of the latter were photographed aiding and encouraging Bolsonaro's rank and file. Instead, members of the *torcidas organizadas* led the effort to break through the barricades in the Brazilian states of Minas Gerais, São Paulo, and Paraná. With an impending Tuesday-night away match against São Paulo FC, for example, members of Atlético Mineiro's Galoucura *torcida* helped clear the roads connecting Belo Horizonte to the metropolis to the southeast. The November 1 game between the hosts and my Clube would, in fact, be played. It ended in a 2–2 draw, naturally, at a time when stalemate appeared to be the order of the day. Less expected was Galo's having made a few new friends along the way, as the fans of other clubs in the Brasileirão took to social media to thank Atlético's supporters for keeping their priorities straight. One of these new fans was the journalist and São Paulo FC supporter Vera Magalhães. "I'm in favour of my team losing to Galo today simply for Galoucura's contribution to [democratic] institutions," Magalhães wrote on Twitter, with a message that was unlikely to endear her to the *Bolsonaristas* who had abused her for her political opinions in the past.[2] This discussion is not to gloss over the rifts in Brazil's politics, which are real, but it is to say that something resembling the carnival spirit that the torcida brings to matchdays in Brazilian futebol played an important part in keeping the lived complications of politics just enough at bay to allow the games of the country's primary domestic competition to continue amid a national crisis that is ongoing. Whether the fans of futebol experienced *felicidade* during this time, let alone alegria, are questions to which not even they might have the answers.

And how could they? The Portuguese term *alegria* is the word Brazilians use to express what is perhaps most inexpressible about the game they love above all others. More than the flicks and tricks of players who possess a certain flair with the ball at their feet, and who provide readymade material for Internet memes these days, the alegria of futebol in Brazil derives from a certain felicity of style in the sport that is also its substance. In his book *Veneno remédio: O futebol e o Brasil* (2008), José Miguel Wisnik locates the source of this style and substance in the contradictions that he inscribes in his work's title. Hilário Franco Júnior points out the paradox contained by the latter, which translates as "Poison Remedy," when he writes that football "is poison and medicine [both], depending on the dosage and the desired effect."[3] By this comment, Franco Júnior would explain that the joy of Brazilian futebol has been at once a boon and a bane to his country's conception of itself. That is, the sport has often been described there as a game of wild oscillations that mirror something inherent in the national character. On the one hand is a "tropically" tinged offensive prowess for which Brazilian players appear to have a particular aptitude. On the other is a defensive absentmindedness that is said to be not only an endemic weakness of the Brazilians' overall play but a fitting figure for the emotional makeup of a country that is supposedly split between unbridled optimism and debilitating pessimism. I read Franco Júnior to mean that the alegria of Brazilian futebol resides for Wisnik in a historically constituted emotional complexity that is somehow part of the very fabric of "being" Brazilian. This view is not to say that Wisnik accepts his country's reputed dual personality as "destiny," as Roberto DaMatta might have it. Rather, Wisnik's suggestion is that the joy of the game of football inheres for Brazilians in their ambivalence about the very legacy of their divided cultural inheritance. "Playfully free and seriously played," Wisnik writes, "football had the ability to reverse the negative dialectic of the vicious circle, converting it into a chain reaction of virtuous ellipses."[4] Brazil's footballers, in other words, have continued to explore the open possibilities of play within a racially segregated, economically ascendant, and class-bound society that they would have every right to consider closed. They've made these explorations in recent years, moreover, while confronting their country's deep-seated political differences as well as the public-safety guidelines associated with COVID-19.

We should not underestimate the impact the pandemic had on Brazilians' capacity to experience alegria in their preferred sport. The game changed under COVID-19, and so did what Norbert Elias might describe as the emotional "atmosphere" that envelops futebol in Brazil.[5] Early in the pandemic, in late May 2020, groups aligned for and against then-President Bolsonaro took to the streets of Belo Horizonte to signal their support for or condemnation of his administrative management of what was clearly more than a medical emergency. Among the detractors who turned out in Minas Gerais's capital were a sizeable showing of futebol fans from all three of Belo Horizonte's top-division sides at the time: Atlético Mineiro, Cruzeiro, and América-MG. Some of these fans (of futebol, not Bolsonaro) represented one or another popular social movement from the period. Among these last were the gig-economy delivery workers, or *entregadores antifascistas*, who organized as a mutual-aid collective after COVID hit. Others belonged to actual political parties, including the newly formed Unidade Popular (UP). And then there were the politically left-leaning members of such *torcidas organizadas* as had rallied around their opposition to what they called the "fascism" of a Bolsonaro government that resisted calls from the populace for a more concerted response to COVID. UP's president, Leonardo Péricles, remarked of the inter-futebol alliance the pandemic forged, "We have rivalry in the field, but we have to be united against fascism and against the threat of dictatorship." Surely the love that Brazilians share for their country's favored game had by this stage transcended the emotional connections and "networks of affection" the torcida provides for countless fans in happier, healthier times.[6]

As for how we might assess the emotional consequences of COVID-19 on futebol, we do know that with the resumption of games at all professional levels during the 2020 and 2021 seasons, footballers' physical performance metrics declined in almost every category of quantitative measurement. Compared to their outputs before the pandemic, players who took to the pitch ran less and for shorter distances, while undertaking fewer accelerations and decelerations than before. No doubt the reduction in recovery times between matches played can account for some of these statistical downturns. Such were the disruptions to the league calendar caused by COVID-19 that athletes found themselves playing the same number of matches as in pre-pandemic seasons, yet at shorter intervals than was the norm. Their performances worsened as a result, as did the average number of goals recorded per match.[7] Of course, we must recall that all this was happening at a moment when the joyful release that typically accompanies the scoring of goals at matches might have gone some way toward improving the emotional lives of people who had been spared from any "serious" COVID-related complaint. To this end, Elias reminds us that play alone cannot be counted on to resolve the buildup of all our emotional tensions.[8] Never having been paid to play football, I furthermore can't fully appreciate how pay-for-play *felt* inside the virtual vacuum that is an empty stadium. Surely, the presence of fans who've shown that they can literally break through political barricades, if necessary, would have made a difference in how players performed. Speaking for myself, I felt nothing like alegria while watching COVID-era matches on television inside the echo chamber of my own living room, where "joy" was in short supply.

Meanwhile, the game itself has quietly suffered over the years from what I would describe as the mixed treatment it's received from academics who struggle with whether and how to address play in their scholarship. Wisnik tackles the issue directly. To those who suppose that studying football with analytical rigor will deprive the sport of its emotional content, he responds, "Football can be a simultaneous object of passion and intellectual challenge."[9] Citing an unpublished essay, "*Lógicas do futebol*," by the late Brazilian philosopher Luiz Sérgio Coelho de Sampaio, Wisnik actually advances a theory of play that offers to turn what he regards as the contradictions of sport to his interpretive advantage when he writes that "football has no logic because it has logics that intersect and dispute, alternate, and complement each other" in ways that a more essentializing perspective on play would prevent us from appreciating.[10] To be clear, Wisnik is no more willing to cede Brazil's internal discussions on sport to those who want to tame futebol—the "*donos do campo*," he calls them—through rules and regulations than he is to the "*donos da bola*" who resist the rigidification of the game for reasons ideological and temperamental. Wisnik prefers to keep the tensions between regulation and improvisation in *play* (120–128). Futebol remains for him what he names a "place beyond ideas," or "*lugar fora das idéias*," even while he recognizes that it is also a discursive space for discussing—indeed, for reenacting—Brazil's most contested questions of race, class, and identity (207, 405, 412). Still, no matter how freighted the game is with the weight of the political significance that we assign it, futebol remains for Wisnik "a case of love at first sight" that affords all Brazilians "a collective, quick and convinced adhesion to the secret possibilities that the game offer[s]" (207).[11] For Wisnik, that game's meaning doesn't cease to be personal and highly emotional, despite also being undeniably political.

As for the feeling of alegria itself, nothing I've learned from the people with whom I spoke while researching and writing this book has convinced me that to *feel* happy is to *be* happy, or that the purpose of playing (football or anything else) is to achieve what we might call "happiness." To extend the (un)reasoning behind Wisnik's futebol "logics" further, I suggest that we needn't have a reason to play in the first place, and that if we did, it would probably represent some combination of thoughts and feelings that were not wholly rational, at least according to the standards of moral philosophers. At the same time, I also suggest that the ludic impulse is probably best characterized as an ironic one, given that the rules we put in place to frame and contain our games seldom manage to render play completely predictable, no more so than our everyday "working" lives.

Joyful Returns

Alegria comes and goes. *Mineiro* author (and reputed *atleticano*) Rosa acknowledges as much when he writes, "There was, once in a while, joy."[12] Notwithstanding its ambiguities, alegria as an emotion started to become somewhat clearer to me once I viewed it in the light of two illustrative episodes from Atlético Mineiro's past, a pair of midcentury homecomings spaced several years apart, to compare with my own leave-taking from Brazil. The earlier of these historical occurrences is far more famous than the later one, which I uncovered during my research for this book. Back in the 1930s, during the first decade of what is properly considered "modern" futebol in Brazil, the Brazilian Football Confederation briefly allowed teams from different states to play against one another, only to dispense with this policy in the 1940s. Galo's travels were thereafter confined to the insular state of Minas Gerais until 1950, after which time the increasing postwar availability of domestic air travel afforded the "team behind the mountains," as Ricardo Galuppo names the side whose authoritative history he's written, greater opportunity to face competition from other states.[13] Clube Atlético Mineiro's (CAM's) ambitions, in fact, reached beyond its own nation. As Galuppo writes, the Clube sought "to honor the name of Minas in the world sports scene."[14] And so, with the added impetus of the country's wanting to recover emotionally from the devastating World Cup loss to Uruguay in July, Atlético embarked on a five-week tour of Europe at the close of 1950, becoming the first Brazilian side since the establishment of professional football there in the 1930s to visit the Continent. Other teams followed in due course.

Between November 1 and December 7, 1950, the Clube played ten matches against such quality opponents as Schalke 04, Rapid Wien, and Anderlecht while completing an itinerary that included stops in West Germany, Austria, Belgium, Luxembourg, and France, where one of Galo's games took place in the French-

Figure 4.1 Atlético became the self-proclaimed "Campeões do Gelo" after the success of their European tour in 1950. (*Courtesy Clube Atlético Mineiro.*)

administered Saar Protectorate that would before long fall under the territorial control of Germany. Even someone who was skeptical about the quality of Brazilian football would have had to admit that Atlético impressed. The Clube won six of its matches and split the remaining fixtures with two ties and two losses, scoring twenty-four goals and conceding eighteen along the way—none of which exorcised Brazil's World Cup demons. But the Clube did earn the distinction of *Campeões do Gelo* (Ice Champions), as Atlético came to be known among its supporters in Minas Gerais due to the wintry conditions in which the team's games were played (Figure 4.1).

Not only did CAM impress while out on the road; to judge from the response the team received from the European attendees who came to watch what was, at the time, a rare exhibition of the Brazilian game, the players from Atlético's squad also demonstrated a version of the sport that would have been anomalous to most locals. The previously named Austrian side Rapid Wien did beat a tired Atlético 3–0 when they played, prompting the reporter who covered the match (the Brazilians' worst performance of the trip) for the Vienna newspaper *Arbeiter-Zeitung* to say that the Clube "had disappointed" in its appearance before an assembled sixty thousand spectators.[15] Atlético nevertheless played elsewhere with what seems to have been a joyful verve. Before the Brazilians arrived in Germany on October 27, CAM's young striker, the childhood runaway Ubaldo, who was left out of the team's travel squad while he completed his mandatory military service in the army, responded to questions from the German newspaper *Hamburger Abendblatt* by boasting, "Brazil's football is very good. The audience will be amazed. We hope that we can beat the opponents with our great technique, speed and a game that the opponents will not see through in its structure so quickly."[16] Atlético by and large delivered on this promise. Rio de Janeiro's *Jornal dos Sports* described the team's tour as a "glorious feat," while Ricardo Diéz, the Clube's Uruguayan manager, proudly told the *Diário de Minas* newspaper upon the heroes' return to a daylong parade and a succession of civic receptions that his "guys play with their hearts and with a love for the shirt of the *alvi-negra*."[17] Such was the excitement that attended the team's trip back to the Minas capital that even *cruzeirenses* turned out at Belo Horizonte's Pampulha airport to greet an Atlético delegation that the writer for *Diário* named "ambassadors" of futebol Brasileiro.[18]

Some of this praise is probably hyperbole and reflects the boastful pride of a people whose cultural horizons were perhaps not as expansive as those of Europeans in the era. Yet more than simply establishing the international "prestige" of the Brazilian game, as the headline in *Diário* announced, Atlético Mineiro's road performances helped introduce the Continent to a style of football that was expressive of feelings that reflected something other than the plodding postwar productivity to which the well-drilled teams of contemporary Europe had been conditioned. Willy Wolf, manager of the Stade Français side that CAM faced in Paris on December 7, singled out the Brazilians' "skillful" passing ability after his team succumbed to Atlético 2–1. The presumed thinking behind the German coach's remarks is that the pass well made is the foundation for a game well played, and he acknowledged afterward that his own French "pupils" were far from capable of producing such a well-executed performance of their own. An unidentified writer from Rio de Janeiro's *O Globo* agreed with this assessment and heaped praise on CAM's players for what he called "their superior technique, ball control, precision and passing stability" against "a strong antagonist."[19] This last could have been either CAM's opponents on the day or the frigid conditions under which the game was staged. Atlético, in any case, had been "brilliant" throughout its stay, in the opinion of *Diário de Minas*, constructing patterns of play that belied the dourness of the local weather.[20]

This anecdote is not to adduce geography as an explanation for players' emotional psychology; it is to say that the athletes who appeared for CAM, by all accounts, had developed a habit of transmitting their emotions into their movements out on the pitch. We have no way of knowing whether those emotions included "joy," as would be the case if Atlético's performances conformed to the sunniest of international stereotypes about the way Brazilians play the game, with a beauty and fluidity that are reputedly unique to them. The results of CAM's matches notwithstanding, we can say that the Belo Horizonte side appears to have conducted itself throughout the duration of its European adventures in a manner of which the folks back home approved. CAM's fans could not have been happier about how their players had expressed themselves.

Among these fans we could include the mineiro "director" of the short home movie *Família e futebol*, from the late 1950s, a surviving fifty-six-second clip of which sits in Belo Horizonte's Arquivo Público Mineiro in testament to the joy of sport.[21] The creator of *Família e futebol* by all appearances shot his film with a jittery handheld camera as he rode passenger in a canvas-covered flat-bed truck along the unpaved roads leading out of Minas Gerais's rural outskirts to the "big" city of Belo Horizonte. This film might be silent, but its wide-eyed receptiveness to experience speaks volumes about the feelings of alegria that Atlético's past and present players never quite managed to articulate while I was within earshot of them. *Família e futebol* begins with vintage period footage of the director's immediate environs in the countryside where he resided. His opening impressions are of sparsely vegetated rolling hills and endless sky. Only a few isolated pedestrians here and there interrupt what are otherwise comparative stretches of emptiness. As the vehicle in which he's riding approaches town, however, our observer tracks the discernible changes in the nearby landscape. Gas stations start to appear (the director's truck, in fact, stops at one, as he captures this momentous occasion on film), along with an increasing number of multistoried buildings. Belo Horizonte at that time remained a modest municipality by today's standards, despite being modern Brazil's first planned city, but it had already embarked upon an intensive phase of industrialization by midcentury.[22] And, as we enter the center of this midsize settlement, with its burgeoning population more than a half million strong, we accordingly meet with mounting evidence of a rational administrative vision of what the Brazil of a not-too-distant future would look like during the next stage of the country's socioeconomic development.[23] The signs of this transition are everywhere to be seen: Broad tree-lined avenues, city parks, and office buildings greet the director as he rolls out of the hinterland and into the grid of "civilization," his camera's eye lingering on the edifice of a totemic Banco do Brasil.

What most holds our cameraman's attention is the sight of what has been his destination all along: Stretching across the street at the "Campo do Atlético" stadium is a banner announcing Sunday's daytime "friendly" futebol match between CAM and a provincial Caratinga F.C. The sign's lettering informs us that a preliminary match is kicking off at 2:30 P.M., with the "principal" match scheduled for 3:50 P.M. We're furthermore told that the combined cost of these fixtures is R$10.00 (approximately US$1.87) for "Cavalheiros" and R$5.00 (approximately US$0.94) for "Estudantes e Senhoritas." But perhaps the most telling detail of all within this memorable mise-en-scène is the excitement inferred by the director himself, given the way he abruptly stops recording the moment he arrives before the gates that he's traveled so far to enter. It is as if our cameraman were reacting to a kind of team victory before the players for either side in the headline match have even broken a sweat. There's more than just plain happiness to be had here, and our director is having it, beside himself and breathless as he is. From the filmmaker's perspective, the trip from country to city undoubtedly would have represented a step forward into cultural relevance—hence the kinetic restlessness of his film, which traces an almost antic journey from sleepy backwater into a dynamic environment, the novelty of which remains fresh for our country traveler. Indeed, Belo Horizonte might as well have been the Eternal City for this pilgrim, so rapt are his impressions of the place. As for the teams and the futebol they played, these seemingly represent for him a total sensorial experience that I'd be inclined to call alegria, if I believed that I had a better interpretive hold on the emotions that the Brazilian game implicitly expects us to associate with the same. My sense is that the artist behind *Família e futebol* learned something about alegria during his stay in the cradle of CAM. So did I, although not as much as I would have liked.

For his part, Atlético's superlative striker Reinaldo told me when we spoke that there were times and places when the most pressing emotional question posed by futebol had less to do with knowing (or better yet, understanding) alegria than it did with being concerned about showing too much of it. To have played the game while making an inappropriate demonstration of joy would have been a sign of disrespect to his opponents, he said.[24] Yet to watch the surviving footage of *o Rei* in action is to witness a dazzlingly meandering instance of emotional play on full display.[25] Reinaldo cuts this way and then that. He volleys the ball over the heads of opponents, turning live competitive matches into private games of keep-away. Time slows and then quickens as the player defies the tick of the clock. The field stretches and then condenses as Atlético's all-timer looks for and locates spaces to play that none of us, not least the opposing defenders, even realize could exist. One would give anything to have been there to ask this *craque* at such joyous moments where he thought that he was going and why his playing with *raça*, chutzpah, alegria, and *amor* was the recommended way of getting there. I suspect that he would have said that his play was instinctive, and I've no doubt that it was on some level. But I also like to think that Reinaldo, as he inched his way toward (and sometimes away from) the opposing team's goal, was showing us the virtues of making the most of our feelings *while we're feeling them*. Whatever our professions, and with the "ball" at our feet and open field in front of us, we have an infinite number of ways to proceed, but really just one thing to do: Play. Reinaldo understood this imperative of play better than most who have ever participated in not just "the" game but any game. It's what made him the player he was. Atleticanos will tell you that it's also what has earned him a place in the hearts and minds of the team's supporters to this day.

Emotional Rescues

Not every feeling in futebol announces itself as loudly as the exuberant grade of alegria that Reinaldo imparted (sometimes despite the player's best intentions) in the on-field "event" that was his body in motion.[26] By remaining with the team for as long as they did, several standout representatives from Atlético Mineiro's past settled into a quieter kind of joyfulness than is maybe implied by the emotional lives of players who, for one reason or another, seem to have been constantly on the move. To be sure, the commitment that Atlético's long-timers showed to the Clube from Belo Horizonte restricted the number of professional transfers they might have made from one club to another during their playing careers. And with this constancy perhaps came fewer opportunities for them to experience the feeling of playing in other pastures. The defender Vantuir played for CAM at the start of his career from 1969 to 1974 and again from 1975 to 1978 before returning to manage Atlético Mineiro between 1993 and 1994 and then once more in 1998. His 507 appearances for the Clube as a player were no mean achievement. Defensive midfielder Wanderley Paiva did move to a succession of different teams after starting his career at Atlético in 1966. The 559 appearances that he made between then and 1975 nevertheless rank him second on the list of most games played for the Clube. That he was born and raised a mineiro surely earns him more than an asterisk in CAM's annals. His close affiliation with the team of his youth meant that the emotions he knew as a player were mostly those of a homebody. And then there's Grapete, the defender who only ever played for CAM as a professional, making 486 appearances for the Clube between 1964 and 1975. Whatever alegria he knew as a player was a feeling that must exist unto itself, alone. Unlike the pedestrian filmmaker Otoni, say, or the *Campeões do Gelo* of Atlético lore, Grapete never had to leave Atlético to appreciate what it meant to love Atlético.

Figure 4.2 Ronaldinho Gaúcho at Clube Atlético Mineiro, tearful alegria, April 3, 2013. (*Photograph by Bruno Cantini.*)

The retired Brazilian playmaker Ronaldinho Gaúcho played in the throes of emotion by comparison, unfair as it is to compare anyone to "Ronaldinho," as he's known. Ronaldinho suited up over the years for various teams in various countries; he signed with Atlético Mineiro only toward the end of his career, in 2012, and remained with the Clube until 2014. Named twice as the world player of the year by football's international governing body—in French, the *Fédération Internationale de Football Association*, or FIFA—Ronaldinho is also alegria incarnate.[27] The player who often wore a smile on his face while he was on the pitch exuded a joy that won him many admirers (Figure 4.2). Dancing with the ball at his feet, his long black hair bouncing to the rhythms of his whirling dervish turns, "Ronnie" with his head up could visualize the intersecting planes of the playing field as well as any footballer this century. And, with his characteristic mischief, looking this way before sidestepping that, he could send the right pass (at the right time) to his teammates as they wandered into open channels that hadn't been there even a split second before. It was hard not to smile just to see it happen, let alone to make it happen. I'd describe the experience of watching these feats performed live on television as a kind of thrilling fulfillment, a feeling that I never came close to knowing while I followed the sport during the pandemic.

It must be said that a defiant quality to Ronaldinho's game made him the competitor he was, and it well suited this native son of the southern Brazilian city of Porto Alegre to carry the happily (or not) contrasting tones of CAM's Jekyll and Hyde jersey. "Joy" as Ronaldinho wore it comprised equal parts acceptance (of the game itself) and rejection of anything and anyone who stood in his path on or off the pitch.[28] Ronaldinho's stardom was such that he did not always feel obligated to perform the "dirty" parts of the game; he didn't track back, his man-to-man marking was slack, and he couldn't be counted on to maintain his zonal positioning when opponents were on the attack. Smile as he might, however, Ronnie let opposing players know that they were in for a fight if they should try to take the ball off him during matches. This is the same player of whom the Clube's former board president Rodolfo Gropen said, "He is a *sweet* person. He never raised his voice to anyone."[29] Nor was Ronaldinho anyone's fool. Signed at age thirty-two by Flamengo, at a point in his career when, according to a writer from *Sports Illustrated*, the state of his play was "in a precipitous decline," Ronaldinho walked out on the São Paulo side that specialized in breaking Galo's heart when the team reneged on the R$1.4 million (approximately US$261,365) a month deal they'd promised him.[30] Freed by mutual consent from that employer, Ronaldinho entered negotiations in June 2012 with Rodolfo Gropen and Atlético's then-president, Alexandre Kalil, to play for CAM. On Ronaldinho's side of the bargaining table, his representatives did most of the talking. On Atlético's, President Kalil spoke for the rest. With the same solicitude he would have shown for his own children, or so Gropen likes to say in a story that he's clearly rehearsed, Kalil stipulated at the decisive meeting in Porto Alegre that Ronaldinho would have no special privileges at the Clube. He would be given a short leash, too. The player who'd developed a reputation for having a taste for the nightlife would get no second chances. And as a capper, Ronnie would earn a monthly salary at CAM of a mere R$300,000 (approximately US$56,000), plus bonus money if the team won (and it did) the Copa Libertadores or Recopa Sudamericana with him on the side. Ronaldinho may have starred in the past for giants of the modern game, such as Paris St. Germain in France and FC Barcelona in Spain, but he would need to keep his ego in check if he were to play for the Clube from Belo Horizonte. When they met, Kalil told Ronaldinho, in the words of a reporter who was privy to their dealings, that he "had two loves in his life, his three children and Atlético."[31] What Kalil was offering the player whom he regarded as a kind of prodigal son was the chance to share in the feelings that complemented what the Clube presents as its family values. Ronaldinho accepted the offer in a milestone signing in the history of Atlético Mineiro.

Turning our conversation toward "joy," I asked Gropen why Atlético so often brought people to tears, the example of Ronaldinho himself having prompted me to pose the question. The attorney smiled in response, more for rhetorical effect, I gathered, than because he was at a loss for words.[32] Ronaldinho himself has never been much of a talker, even though he has earned a reputation for being unafraid to express his emotions in public. More to the point, the tears that Ronaldinho famously shed upon entering and exiting the Clube add a wrinkle to the joyful feelings that alegria is supposed to represent in the Brazilian game. President Kalil informed the player when signing him that Ronnie would have to feel the love of atleticanos before he could know what he had enlisted in, emotionally speaking, when he consented to join the side.[33] This knowledge came more quickly than Ronaldinho could have thought possible, for after only a few weeks into his stay at Atlético, in July 2012, the player stood and watched as the team's home supporters raised a banner in his honor at the end of a scoreless draw against Grêmio, the Porto Alegre side where he'd started his career. Fronting that banner was an image of Ronaldino's mother, Miguelina, who was recovering from cancer, and above which was written "Faith in God."[34] The gesture was enough to cause Ronaldinho to cry during the postgame press conference, at which he remarked, "It made me very happy to see the affection they [the supporters] gave me."[35] That these were tears of "happiness," and not sorrow, is significant, since it was usually Ronnie who put fans in touch with their emotions, not the other way around. Here, the emotional roles had been switched.

After he left the Clube in 2014, Ronaldinho cried again, this time at the announcement of his signing with the Mexican side Querétaro in a deal that reportedly marked a sharp increase in the wages he'd been earning at CAM. "For us, he's Ronaldinho Mineiro," President Kalil maintained when asked how he felt about losing a player whom he had worked so hard to bring to the Clube in the first place. For his part, Ronnie tried to keep things positive, saying, "For me these Atlético fans are eternal. It's not goodbye. . . . It's see you soon."[36] True to his word, the player later hinted at a possible return to the Clube while visiting with the team at halftime during CAM's away match in 2015 at the Maracanã against Fluminense. Ronnie instead spent part of that season, the last of his career, suiting up for this same carioca outfit; there would not be another Atlético homecoming for Ronaldinho. The Clube had rescued him before; it would not be rescuing him again. Nor would Dona Miguelina live to see her son in a world without COVID-19, the player's mother having passed away from that disease in February 2021 after falling ill the preceding December.[37] Such is the emotional range of play that's suggested by alegria. As the careers of CAM's players show, futebol can bring unbridled joy today and unspeakable sorrow tomorrow.

Final Tallies

At least one scholar describes Brazil as having been founded on principles of what he calls "ontological excess," the result of early-modern Luso-Brazilian encounters there involving the Old World's "discovery" of the sensory abundance of the "New."[38] Minas Gerais itself, we know, was settled in the early eighteenth century amid the fever of a gold rush that resulted in the province's many "mines." Thus, there are historical reasons why there would be a stronger cultural tradition of "more" futebol and feeling in modern Brazil than "less." Football may once have been a rarity in the country; the sport was invented by Mesoamericans in antiquity before being imported into Brazil in its recognized form by British migrants in the late nineteenth century. Yet football's subsequent re-exportation from Brazil has since confirmed its current surplus status there as an "industry" with parts to spare, while also contributing, some commentators would say, to the attendant lessening of futebol's joy.[39] No more "the beauty that blossoms from the joy of play," Eduardo Galeano mourns of a sport that now saturates world media coverage like no other.[40] Indeed, the pressures that occur during matches today are so palpable that alegria may have become something of a luxury for the players.[41]

At CAM, alegria still *feels* like something that's the result of addition rather than subtraction. We might find one illustrative instance of this claim in the story that's generally accepted as an explanation for how another of the Clube's core emotional contradictions, raça, came into being. The tale traces to the mineiro writer and journalist Roberto Drummond, who is credited with coining the popular Atlético expression, "If there is a black and white shirt hanging on the line during a storm, *atleticano* roots against the wind."[42] The poetic meaning behind the line—and it is poetry, containing as it does an arresting image that demands that we perceive our worlds anew—is that CAM is the side that offers resistance even against as formidable an opponent as nature itself. Reaching back (in time and attribution) further, we know that Drummond crafted his lines after reworking a memorable scene from the early days at the Clube, a time when the team's laundress used to hang the players' uniforms out to dry on a clothesline at the old stadium in Lourdes. The plot twist in this evocative account of a Rooster's being born is that a sudden rain and gust of wind one day is supposed to have sent the washerwoman rushing out to gather the clothes from her line, while a group of reporters, Drummond included, who'd gathered to attend the players' training session watched from under the cover of the stands. With all the shirts but one having been reclaimed, the assembled spectators began to root for the lone jersey that was left hanging to face the wind on its own, a competitive mismatch of almost Biblical proportions. The incident, in turn, came to stand for something essential in the Clube's identity, a determined preparedness to fight under any conditions.[43] As I interpret this metonymic tale of the symbolic shirt, something essentially joyful seems to exist in Atlético's readiness to take on all comers, no matter how many obstacles stand in its way. I would guess that most of us can remember a time when we had no greater joy than to play in the rain.

Or, maybe that's amor. CAM's willingness to always go one better could also be interpreted as the kind of romantic emotion (as opposed to emotional "romance") that I have described in this study. For the Romantics of the late eighteenth and early nineteenth centuries, emotional "excess" has often been characterized as a kind of compensation for the seeming deficiencies in feeling afforded by the rational empiricism that held sway during the Enlightenment.[44] I do not propose that the Clube's Rooster is an arch Romantic, but I do suppose that Galo is best known for nursing feelings that breed more feelings, multiplying emotions rather than dividing them. I maintain this position even if my Clube is no *"Frente de Alegria,"* to borrow the name that the former Brazilian footballer Afonsinho used for the organization he formed in the early 1970s to advocate for players' rights as free agents.[45] Afonsinho's alegria resonated politically, and no doubt financially, for the players whose interests he defended with noteworthy success. The alegria that informs this chapter, and this book, has more to do with the *emotional* components of play.

Whether *That Futebol Feeling* comprises one of the "counter-narratives of Latin America, its history, development, and modernity" that two scholars have called for in the discipline of Latin American studies, I leave for others to decide.[46] I do know that I've tried to tell a story about Brazilian society and sport that not only crosses academic disciplines but combines them in ways that make this book multidisciplinary in the best sense of the word. To this extent, you might say that I've aspired to write in what one student of the game calls *"na gramática do futebol"* (in the grammar of football), with an eye toward capturing on the page emotions that would perhaps not be fully registered had I relied on more formal and customary uses of language, arrangement, and representation[47]—hence my evident fondness for vernacular forms of expression as well as the moments of journalistic play-by-play, free association, and first-person chronicle that structure my account.

At the same time, I need there to be no mistaking the fact that I set out with this book to complete a project that was not only fun to research and write but also to read. That I've placed my scholarly reputation, such as it is, on the line while doing so says a lot about the conditions under which scholars labor today. I'd work harder if I thought that it would help reduce the degree of self-consciousness that I felt while applying myself so joyfully to a book "about" play.

This statement is not to suggest that I resolved the problem (I didn't) of how to disentangle politics from the scholarship on sport. Nor have I been able (I haven't) to figure out how to conclude an account that is ongoing. My sense is that football's definitive story must wait to be written so long as there are more games to be played. Happily, there are. So, I leave things hanging in the balance by writing about the feelings I was experiencing as the calendar turned to August 2022, when I still had a few weeks to go before leaving Belo Horizonte.

The prospects of Atlético Mineiro's season at that moment were as follows. On Sunday, July 31, the team's away trip to Porto Alegre to face Internacional at the Beira-Rio stadium could not have resulted in a worse outcome. A newly reinstalled Cuca's first match at the helm of the Clube that he led to Brasileirão glory in 2021 ended in a 3–0 defeat, with Atlético shipping all three goals in the game's opening half hour. This experience didn't feel like joy, and if it was love, then it was a "cold shower," as one reporter quipped.[48] The changes to the side that Cuca made at halftime provided some faint hope that the team could mount the comeback that never came. Atlético was left sitting seventh in the league table with twenty matches played and another eighteen still to complete by November 13.[49] My friend Luiz Silva captured the feelings of supporters at this interval with the clever neologism *Galotapisanotomat*, his Portuguese-English mashup for a very disappointed Rooster.[50]

Luiz was also right about Atlético's being a "weird team," bracing itself as it did for the most challenging fixtures while sometimes failing to prepare adequately (and emotionally) for the more winnable ones.[51] That weirdness could have boded well for the coming Wednesday's Copa Libertadores quarterfinal home game against league leaders Palmeiras. Atlético needed to bring their A game if they were to stand a chance in this all-Brazilian encounter, or at least give themselves a foothold in the tie ahead of the next week's away leg in São Paulo. Yet Atlético conceded a late goal in the opening leg to level things 2–2 before allowing no fewer than three second-half goals in the home-league loss to Athletico Paranaense that weekend, on August 7. This outcome meant that CAM had it all to do in the second-leg Copa match against Palmeiras, on what proved to be a rainy Wednesday night on August 10, 2022. I had been invited to the penthouse apartment of "cultural producer" Afonso Borges to watch the match with some other new Galo acquaintances in Belo Horizonte. These included the futebol journalist Chico Maia, who writes for the Belo Horizonte daily *Hoje em Dia*; photographer Eugênio Sávio, renowned for his stunning still-image coverage of eight World Cups; and musician Celso Adolfo, who, as part of the Minas Gerais–originated Clube da Esquina artists collective, had his debut album *Coração Brasileiro* (1983) produced by Grammy Award–winning artist Milton Nascimento. I was as likely to be swept off my feet by this talented assemblage of people as I was by the wind, which whipped across our upper-deck party as a portent of worse things to come. As for the match, it remained scoreless at halftime, despite Palmeiras having a player sent off in the twenty-ninth minute. Atlético pressed in the opening sections of the second half without scoring the goal that would have seen them through to the tournament's semifinals, from which stage they might have reprised the Copa Libertadores "miracle" that saw them bring home the tournament's coveted trophy in 2013. After Palmeiras had yet another player dismissed with a red card in the eighty-second minute, the Rooster was in the catbird seat, for Atlético was left facing an undermanned side—yet none of this mattered in the end. With neither side having scored, the outcome was left to be decided on penalties, and, painful as it is to record, Atlético Mineiro faltered, with Palmeiras taking the shootout 6–5 after CAM substitute Rubens's tame effort rolled harmlessly into the hands of the home team's keeper.

It was close to midnight by then. After speaking to guitarist Adolfo earlier in the evening, I'd been thinking about the six-string COVID-19 instrument I had acquired in March 2020, as I tried, like many people, to find an emotional outlet during a lockdown that had hurt more than just my feelings. I had hoped that Celso might ask me whether I played—the guitar, that is. My response was ready: "Mostly when I work," I would have said, since that's the mind-set I try to adopt whenever I undertake what is otherwise my chosen form of gainful employment. The morning after the Copa Libertadores match, the Clube posted on its Instagram page the stirring speech that Cuca had delivered to the team right before the previous evening's defeat. He had left no doubt in the players' minds that they were there, as he had said, "to be champion" and that "it's with raça that you win." The manager had every reason to want to dispel any doubts from the players' minds; it was his job to convince them of the practical and emotional impossibility of losing. But I could not help but read something else into Cuca's words when he had stated, "We are not here for nothing."[52] Winning is nice, of course, but surely there is meaning in simply having a hand (and a foot) in the games we play, however we play them. Sávio had encapsulated his own feelings about CAM's exit from the Copa with a softly spoken "*Futebol é uma merda*," which translates idiomatically as "Football sucks." I was not in the mood then to disagree. In retrospect, however, it did occur to me to remind myself that "joy," as I understand it, is less an absolute condition than a comparative one. Were it not for the setbacks, alegria wouldn't mean much.

The results of Atlético's remaining fixtures for the 2022 season have been written by now. They are part of the sporting record to which I have done my best to contribute with the volume that you are finishing. As for myself, I've moved on to other projects. Looking back on my residence in Brazil, I can recognize how emotional a time my four months there were. It's hard for me not to smile when I recall the elation of my arrival, for example, or the excitement of my settling in and the nervous anticipation that I always feel before I teach a new class. Then followed the unavoidable feeling of separation from the places and people who represent my everyday existence in the United States. I was glad to step away from these familiarities for a spell, I must admit, yet I found it hard to replace them, knowing that my time in Minas Gerais was so short. I'd signed on to stay in Belo Horizonte long enough to take a break from my "American" routines, but not nearly long enough to be able to establish a foothold in the place where I would be living and working over the course of a New England summer that transpired without me. I must admit that I did become a bit frustrated on occasion while living abroad because of feeling (and being) so un-Brazilian in my regimented personal habits. I also confess to growing weary from time to time after taking too many Uber trips to and from the university where I taught. These feelings are unexceptional, I realize, despite the personal significance that my time in Brazil retains for me.

I am sure that the months I spent in Minas Gerais devoting myself to CAM taught me a great deal about the emotional side of the games we play. There may be no English equivalent for the state of being that is raça. Amor might not be synonymous with the widespread love for the sport that I have described in these pages. And alegria does not always manifest in the ways and means that we think it will. The emotions that move us when- and wherever we experience them are no less "real," however, because of their regional Brazilian variations than they would be if we all felt uniformly. I think and believe that our capacity for feeling differently may even be what makes us most human and why we keep reading about such feelings in books like this one. An "American" by birth, a mineiro by association, I felt and still feel like an atleticano at age fifty and counting precisely because I've been carried away by my feelings on occasion. I would not have it any other way.

I hope readers take away from *That Futebol Feeling* a reimagined sense of what it means to work and play in this world, whether we're students of sport, fans of world football, or people who think that politics needs to compete with play as a kind of prerequisite for responsible purposefulness. I very much want to believe that books like this one can help restore play to what I suggest is its rightful place in our day-to-day lives. If I believed that play was a place apart, I'd be tempted to go there to stay. But that's not why I traveled to Brazil, any more than it is the reason why I returned to the United States. I'd prefer that we not insist on locating play somewhere outside the delimited area that it seems we've allotted for "seriousness." I have likewise avoided a tendency to regard play as being as nonpurposeful (and even as pleasurable) as we've been led to think that it should be by the dictates of custom and convention. I'd rather have play be something that we carry with us, no matter whether we're fighting or loving or simply feeling.

Appendix

That Futebol Feeling: Sport and Play in Brazil's Heartland is as much "about" the emotional meanings of *futebol* in a particular Brazilian state as it is the different approaches that are available for thinking and writing about sport. Accordingly, this appendix explains the methods I've used in the research and writing of this book. It also contextualizes the special methodological considerations I faced in bringing *That Futebol Feeling* to completion.

Among the most important is the book's high level of reflexiveness. A quick perusal of *That Futebol Feeling* could lead readers to decide that it's a "passion project," a phrase that academics reserve for any undertaking that's animated more by a scholar's unthinking enthusiasm for his or her subject matter than by the disciplinary rigors and consensual standards of "serious" scholarship in one's chosen field(s) of inquiry. I address the passionate nature of all sports in the body of this book, yet the project at hand raises a "meta" dilemma that invites further mention here. On the one hand, I confess that I am passionate about the Brazilian futebol team that I support, the historic Belo Horizonte side Clube Atlético Mineiro (CAM). On the other, I have deliberately made the passion for sport among Atlético's supporters a focal point of attention throughout *That Futebol Feeling*. All of which is to say that my own passion for this project has informed my attempts to interrogate the complex meanings that attach to the passion that fans of CAM reserve for their team within the Brazilian state of Minas Gerais and beyond. The highly self-referential nature of the investigative situation that results from this book's overlapping orientations is not unlike what epistemological philosophers must face whenever they think about thinking, or what labor historians reckon with when they perform the difficult work of archival research. Both of these last examples are germane to this present study, for I do have strong feelings about the feelings that sport can inspire within a given culture, and I'm serious about the work that's required to contemplate the cultural significance of *play* when it takes the form of sport.

I've been aided greatly in my work by the precedents set by comparable projects. Foremost among these is the Trinidadian-born C. L. R. James's book on cricket, *Beyond a Boundary* (1963). Immersed as he was (as a player and as a print journalist) in the game he writes about so incisively, James composes what remains one of the foundational studies of the relationship between sport and culture. Those who are familiar with James's work will see that, like James, I have similarly immersed myself in my project, albeit as someone who was never likely to make the grade as a professional athlete and who has never been paid for sports punditry. These differences notwithstanding, I also adopt, as James does, a first-person perspective for those portions of this book that I present as a personal narrative of sorts. A more recent model of scholarship in this same vein that I have followed is Grant Farred's *Long Distance Love: A Passion for Football* (2008). Written for the "Sporting" series of Temple University Press, this book proceeds in its author's inimitable fashion to examine Farred's "passion" for England's Liverpool Football Club. His methodological posture recalls James's, committed as both writers are to a thoroughgoing assessment of the political, postcolonial importance of organized sports in the transatlantic region. Like James and Farred, I, too, have tried to establish with *That Futebol Feeling* an intellectual ground on which those who are passionate about sport and other recognized forms of play can pursue their projects without having to apologize for their emotional investment in their work. And I am happy to report that as much as I have benefitted from the example of both writers in this regard, I have done so without experiencing the anxiety of influence that might otherwise accompany a debt that I openly acknowledge.

In fact, I am comfortable enough with my borrowings from James and Farred to offer some resistance to the two-part Jamesian assumption (subscribed to by Farred, up to a point) that I argue superintends the academic study of society and sport today. The crux of this assumption is that all sports have political significance, and thus sports commentators carry an obligation to deal with politics in some way if they want their work to be properly heard. I resist this assumption, as I say, yet I make my demurral knowing that certain readers might look with suspicion upon my willingness to treat "passion," emotion, and play as being outside the bounds of politics per se. This admission is not to suggest that I'm ready

to accept any form of cultural expression as evidence of whichever interpretive assertions I want to make; rather, I believe politics to be but one
of the many ends of analysis for those who write about sports. To be
clear, my claim is that the comparative playfulness that characterizes my
approach (compared to the seeming seriousness of politics, that is) can
be read as a symptom of this book's having been written in a mood that
recalls the open emotionalism of *Beyond a Boundary* and *Long Distance
Love*. All three books are generic hybrids. Each of them maintains the
critical distance that we associate with secondary scholarship, even while
their authors' sincere, if ironically self-aware, handling of primary source
materials adds a heightened emotional dimension to our understanding
of what counts as empirical "proof" in the first place. With that said, I
can't pretend to have altogether avoided offering political explanations of
my own from time to time in *That Futebol Feeling*. Indeed, my relative
failures in this regard amount to something of a subplot in these pages,
where my best intentions have been complicated, if not compromised, by
the weight of writerly convention.

Readers might well ask why I didn't write a futebol novel instead.
The comparative freedoms of fictional narrative could have insulated me
from the potential objections of scholars who have every right to expect
the authors of expository prose to conform to the usual rules of academic
writing. And, to be fair, I can't deny that my monograph draws on certain
elements of the long-story form, enough so to give some indication that
this book aspires to be the work of fiction that it's decidedly not. A plot
unfolds herein, as I've already suggested by alluding to the conflicts of a
political/methodological "subplot." This study has an explicit theme, too,
which reveals itself through the manifold images and leitmotifs of work
and play that circulate throughout the whole. *That Futebol Feeling* also
features an assortment of "characters" who are represented by the people whom I interviewed and read about during the research stage of this
project. Even the epigraphs that I have chosen for my individual chapter
headings derive from a belletristic strain of world literature, the authors
of these passages having evinced a particular interest in sport. Unlike a
novelist, however, I'm not especially interested in exploring how our felt
impressions of the world "play" on the page. I have proceeded, rather,
with the aim of combining the kinds of insights afforded by our feelings
with the knowledge we gain through our rational engagement with "problems" that don't have definitive solutions. Not only does conventional
scholarly analysis strike me as being inadequate to the interpretive task of
explaining something as amorphously "fun" as play; any effort to account
for how we feel about feelings that is, itself, unfelt somehow feels wholly
inappropriate to me. In any case, the feelings of the persons (including
myself) whom I have written about are no more imaginary than the people

themselves are. Thus, I have consciously avoided composing a fiction that, I believe, would only serve to render as a fanciful abstraction my determination to make the emotional work of weighing the emotions something that any of us can try on terms that extend the traditional boundaries of the essay form and critical nonfiction. The promiscuous style and substance of *That Futebol Feeling* should not be mistaken for a methodological corrective to "normal" sports writing. What this book wants to be is a "playful" provocation for anyone who is emotionally stirred by sport to reconsider why this should be so.

I am hardly a pioneer in this regard. My work leans on the example of scholars who made (and continue to make) play a subject of purposeful academic inquiry by questioning the operative methodologies of their respective disciplines. American cultural anthropologist Clifford Geertz is one such scholar. *That Futebol Feeling* may not achieve the same level of "thick description" that Geertz has made famous in his studies of the richly symbolic cultural life of "primitive" societies in Indonesia. As much as I was able to learn about *atleticanos'* playful behaviors during my four-month Fulbright residence in Belo Horizonte, Brazil, I probably would have required a research stay approaching something closer to four years before I could have been able to offer up cultural descriptions as dramatically detailed as Geertz's. Still, this book does pay homage to Geertz's concept (borrowed from English social theorist Jeremy Bentham) of "deep play," which the former defines as a form of play "in which the stakes are so high that it is . . . irrational for men to engage in it at all."[1] That my observations of CAM's inanimate rooster mascot, Galo, should recall Geertz's own observations of Balinese cockfights in the late 1950s is thus no coincidence, indebted as I am to my American predecessor's model for "reading" a society's gaming culture as an extension of its everyday experiences. Nor should the unspoken parallel that I draw between two very different scenes of cockfighting/playing be taken with just an ironic wink and a nod, for I owe much to Geertz's appreciation of how a culture's *deepest* feelings can manifest in play. "THE DEEPER THE MATCH," Geertz explains, in what he characterizes as an interpretive departure from "functionalist" sociology, "the greater the emotion that will be involved and the more the general absorption in the match" (22, 26). Nothing better captures than this last statement the premise of my project on futebol.

I also take inspiration from Dutch cultural historian Johan Huizinga. Huizinga's book *Homo Ludens: A Study of the Play-Element in Culture* (1938) may place him in what anthropologist Roberte Hamayon calls the "generalist camp" of cross-cultural play studies that's occupied by the Dutchman and his like-minded successor, French intellectual Roger Caillois. By comparison, the localized "microhistory" of the emotions I've written about futebol in Brazil's Minas Gerais state aligns me with a particularist tradition within the discipline instead.[2] These differences in scale and orientation notwithstanding, I take heart from Huizinga's willingness to attend to the morphologies of play across a range of imaginative fields of endeavor, including literature, the arts, and religion, to name only a few of the cultural arenas in which his understanding of play *plays*, without betraying any sense that he feels a personal or professional need to speak to more "serious" subjects, such as economics, politics, and a conventional variety of institutional history.[3] Indeed, Huizinga conceives of all adult forms of play as being separate from "seriousness," without discounting politics as such in his work and without ceasing to take play seriously enough for it to warrant scrutiny. Huizinga looks upon politics as *"symptomatic rather than causative,"* as one of the historian's recent commentators summarizes, and I like to think that I have assumed a similar perspective in *That Futebol Feeling*.[4] And although I do not quite share Huizinga's stated belief that "the *fun* of playing, resists all analysis" (*Homo Ludens* 3), I have often found myself falling into Huizinga's habit of conveying my ideas on play in contrary terms. Much as Huizinga explains play by explaining what it's *not* (play is a "culture-creating function" that's not "serious," he says), I've found it all but impossible to propose a working alternative to the scholarly conventions of writing about play without invoking those same conventions by way of negative reference (*Homo Ludens* 179).[5] This appendix is but another instance of the "meta" properties of my project, then, which is only fitting when we recall that other scholars (Geertz included) likewise think about play as a reflexive way of framing cultural expression generally.[6] Hamayon proposes her own "negative definition" of play when she remarks that "'playing' does not present itself as a true 'doing,' but can, however . . . constitute 'a kind of' doing."[7] I've conducted a comparable kind of balancing act with *That Futebol Feeling*, playfully recognizing/not recognizing play as what Michael Puett calls "a fundamental way of human acting in the world" while recording the complexities of that world by using methods that amount to a self-conscious study in contrasts.[8]

The gist of that contrast is this: On the one hand, I see myself as having written *That Futebol Feeling* in the tradition of such scholars as Huizinga, Geertz, and "macro" sociologist Norbert Elias, who each approach play in a spirit of opposition to a prevailing tendency among their contemporaries in the twentieth century to "depreciate" play, as Hamayon says, as something that's not "serious."[9] On the other hand, I have felt at times while working on this project that scholars who take play seriously today perhaps take it *too* seriously, at least for my purposes. Within the sports-related fields of anthropology, sociology, and ethnography in which I'm *not* trained as a specialist, the burden of proof for the argument that play is something other than "silly" has rested heavily on the shoulders of those who would likely sympathize, in principle, with the outlines of my interest in Brazilian futebol.[10] But in practice, and as someone whose first loyalties are to the "textually" dependent and emotionally sensitive modes of representation and knowledge production associated with the humanities, my disciplinary commitment to "empirical" evidence is different from that of my counterparts in the social sciences, even though I am just as invested as they are in earning play a seat at the table of "serious" scholarly discussion.[11] For my part, my own methodological approach to play proceeds from a belief that the feelings play conjures in "players" are no more easily controlled within the cultures that create them—a claim with which Elias himself would surely have agreed—than they are by the scholars who assume the task of treating these feelings "seriously."[12] I may not maintain the same relationship to "data" as Hamayon does, but I agree with her that one of the essential "effects" of play is to "curve empirical realities" just enough to blur the distinction between the "fictional framework created by the player" and the so-called actual world that exists outside the agreed-upon domains of play.[13] As for that "actual" world, Eduardo P. Archetti (who urges that play "be taken seriously by anthropologists") reminds us that it's not only composed of the professional athletes who are paid to play but also includes the "shallow players" who follow sports as spectators, as well as the scholars who, historically, have helped make play what Archetti describes as "a key arena for the analysis of the way individuals 'play' with modernity and the complexity of self-awareness."[14] It's precisely this "self-awareness" that has left me, at least, always already implicated (as I insist that I should be) in the most emotional aspects of my subjects of study. By design, *That Futebol Feeling* has made this methodological "self-awareness" part of its overarching argument.

Of course, one of the dangers that a person faces in adopting a "meta" method in his or her research on play is the aforementioned potential for control bias this approach poses. Feeling as passionately as I do about CAM, I run the risk of being too deeply attached to my topic to notice that I may have failed to apprehend it with a suitable level of *dispassion*. Yet the circumstances surrounding my project have gone some way toward safeguarding me from what many would perceive to be the professional hazards of conducting research in which the scholar him- or herself participates as an "object" of inquiry. To begin, several recent works of sports scholarship have afforded me a convenient, theoretically informed illustration of what qualifies as an appropriate amount of immersion in the scholarly pursuit of play. Douglas Hartmann's *Midnight Basketball: Race, Sports, and Neoliberal Social Policy* (2016) is one such book, attuned as it is to what the author characterizes as Americans' "paradoxical orientation toward sport, wherein folks exhibit tremendous passion for sport . . . but also minimize sport as 'just a game' not to be taken too seriously."[15]

Another such work is Ugo Corte's "ethnography" of big wave surfing on the North Shore of Hawai'i's O'ahu, *Dangerous Fun: The Social Lives of Big Wave Surfers* (2022). Not only does Corte portray play, like fun, as "autotelic, meaning that it depends on the willingness of participants to engage in it to no particular end other than satisfaction"; like Hartmann, he recognizes that what Corte calls the "emotional engagement" of play is subject to a kind of force multiplier effect "through its subsequent narrative iterations." In other words, a "fun residue" is involved whenever we tell (and retell) the story of play after the fact, creating feelings to which not even scholars who have been trained to regard sport as something other than "trivial" are immune.[16]

Speaking of contagion, the impact that COVID-19 had on my research methods was significant, to be sure.[17] The emotional interest of my project required me to situate myself as closely as possible to the cultures of play surrounding CAM. Those were the conditions that would best facilitate the writing of my own idiosyncratic version of what Michael DeLand terms "a close-up ethnographic study."[18] But the imperatives of my research did not always correspond to the health and safety protocols that were in place in the city of Belo Horizonte during my stay there between May and September 2022. CAM's games continued to be played during this interval in stadiums that were often full. I attended several of these matches in person: a rewarding kind of immersive research. CAM's world-class training facilities nevertheless remained closed to me, despite my appeals for "scholarly" access to the players at the site of their most frequent (and most informal) associations with each other. The local journalists who worked for outlets other than the team's in-house GaloTV network suffered a similar ban, so I was not the only interested party prevented from speaking with current players in a relatively relaxed setting on nongame days. That my predicament was the same as what others were enduring offered me little consolation, however, and I resorted by necessity to speaking with former and current players alike through the remote Zoom conferences I conducted with them online while I was in-country. The situation was different (as it was, say, with CAM's renowned striker Reinaldo) whenever the stature of the individual involved allowed for in-person alternatives, or when interviewees proved interested enough in my work to invite me to sit down with them for a face-to-face meeting (duly masked, naturally) in a neutral, prearranged setting. The global reach of the Clube's appeal meant that online interviews with supporters, sports commentators, and football writers and filmmakers were the only logical option when a respondent was based in another city, or even another country. In any case, establishing a too-intimate proximity to my topic proved to be less of a problem with this project than the everyday exigencies of the pandemic. I was simply incapable of becoming overly immersed in my research situation, a circumstance that no amount of scholarly persuasion could change. Then again, these difficulties of access served as encouragement for me to further augment the sources from which I collected my "data," which ended up deriving from a rewardingly diverse pool of interviewees. It had never been my intention to restrict my interactions with the cultures of CAM to the meetings I arranged with the active squad members who appeared in games for Atlético during the season when I visited Brazil. The fallout from COVID-19 ensured that I made good on this intention, more so than I ever could have anticipated as I waited through not one but two deferrals (encompassing the COVID summers of 2020 and 2021) for the start date of my Fulbright residence in Brazil.

In the end, *That Futebol Feeling* tests the boundaries of play in ways that not even (or, especially) its most "serious" students will likely approve. I'm not as convinced as others are that play is always voluntary; as with COVID-19, play can sometimes be "catching." I don't believe that play must occur within fixed limits of time or space, either, not least when we stipulate that play can exist only outside the conventionally accepted parameters of our "ordinary" working lives. For me, the rules that we have or haven't written for play when it takes the form of sport or sports scholarship aren't as binding as we might have been conditioned to think. Indeed, play can sometimes be "unthinking"; or, as is the case with this book, play might combine with "work" in such a way as to suggest new rules for when, where, and how "play" can proceed. If play can't be forced, it's always felt, and play's aims as an action or even as an attitude are reciprocal in the sense that the purpose of play is itself, which is to say "play." Play can be pleasurable. Play should be fun, and, as Corte observes, fun is a feeling of "collective" pleasure that's experienced in groups and "extends beyond mere satisfaction, comforting embodiment, or agreeable affect."[19] The fun that play often produces makes a people, in the sense that it builds and sustains allegiances between individuals who might otherwise have no ostensible reason to associate but for what Randall Collins describes as the "micro-dynamics of emotion as a social process."[20] I had much fun in writing this book, and my hope is that others experience something similar upon reading it, whatever might be the differences in our views on sport.

Notes

Chapter 1

1. Roberte Hamayon, *Why We Play: An Anthropological Study*, trans. Damien Simon (2012; rept. Chicago: HAU Books, 2016), 13–14, 18–20; Ugo Corte, *Dangerous Fun: The Social Lives of Big Wave Surfers* (Chicago: University of Chicago Press, 2022), 81; and Susan Birrell, "Sport as Ritual: Interpretations from Durkheim to Goffman," *Social Forces* 60, no. 2 (December 1981): 354–355.

2. Michael Atkinson comments on the noticeable surge in general scholarly production that the academy has witnessed in the aftermath of COVID-19 in his chapter "Interview(s) with the Vampire: Research Opportunism during a Global Catastrophe," in *Sport and Physical Culture in Global Pandemic Times*, ed. David L. Andrews, Holly Thorpe, Joshua I. Newman (London: Palgrave Macmillan, 2023), 771–795.

3. In *Brazil's Dance with the Devil: The World Cup, the Olympics, and the Fight for Democracy* (Chicago: Haymarket Books, 2014), sportswriter Dave Zirin goes so far as to maintain that football in Brazil has developed into a "neoliberal game" overseen by "oligarchic powers" (131, 133).

4. Ademar Crosara Junior, "A identificação com o time, a curiosidade específica do torcedor e a satisfação do torcedor como antecedentes da intenção de compra do torcedor de futebol no Brasil" (Dissertação, Programa de Pós-graduação em Administração, Universidade Federal de Uberlândia, 2016), 50.

5. The gravity of games should not be underestimated. Since ancient times, games have served their players as a representation of man's struggle

for life and death. See Johan Huizinga, *Homo Ludens: A Study of the Play-Element in Culture* (1938; rept. London: Routledge, 2003), 3, 4, 16. Marcelino Rodrigues da Silva addresses the theoretical question of whether a game like football can "function," he writes, "as a system of meaning capable of referring to meanings outside its referential universe." In this author's view, it can. From Rodrigues da Silva's "O mundo do futebol e a crônica esportiva," *FuLiA* 2, no. 3 (2018): 91–92, 97. For a comparable view on football's potential meaningfulness within a global context, see Hilário Franco Júnior, *A dança dos deuses: Futebol, cultura, sociedade* (São Paulo: Companhia das Letras, 2007), 166.

6. Holly Thorpe, Joshua I. Newman, and David L. Andrews (Eds.), "Introduction: Assembling COVID/COVID Assemblages," in *Sport and Physical Culture in Global Pandemic Times*, 6.

7. According to Martha de Ulhôa Carvalho, "One of the characteristics of Brazilians is their fondness for puns and word play." From Carvalho's "Canção da América—Style and Emotion in Brazilian Popular Song," *Popular Music* 9, no. 3 (October 1990): 331.

8. Hamayon, *Why We Play*, 14–17; and Thierry Wendling, *Ethnologie des joueurs d'échecs* (Paris: Presses Universitaires de France, 2002), 29.

9. Simon Kuper and Stefan Szymanski announce the emergence of football as a "numbers game" in *Soccernomics: Why England Loses, Why Germany and Brazil Win, and Why the U.S., Japan, Australia, Turkey—And Even Iraq—Are Destined to Become the Kings of the World's Most Popular Sport* (New York: Nation Books, 2009), 4–6.

10. Biographical writing about players greatly influenced the development of modern sports culture in Brazil in the early decades of the twentieth century. Marcelino Rodrigues da Silva examines the nature of this body of writing in "Guará, o craque que não foi: Ficção e história na biografia esportiva," *Aletria* 26, no. 3 (2016): 157–174. Umberto Eco similarly stipulates that football can indeed be "a game played in the first person" and thus viewed from players' perspectives rather than reduced to a media spectacle that is staged exclusively for the sake of an audience. See Eco's "Sports Chatter" (1969), in *Travels in Hyperreality: Essays*, trans. William Weaver (New York: Harcourt Brace Jovanovich, 1986), 161.

11. Huizinga, *Homo Ludens*, 199.

12. Marcelino Rodrigues da Silva identifies the sports *chronicle*, or *crônica esportiva*, as a "hybrid" literary genre in Brazil with roots in the nineteenth-century feuilletons of Paris. He locates the genre somewhere between the empirical journalistic coverage of professional sports and a discursive "space" (often, but not always, located in the same Brazilian newspapers and magazines that report football facts) where "the interpretation of football finds itself free for higher flights." From Rodrigues da Silva's "O mundo do futebol e a crônica esportiva," 97–98.

13. By way of comparison, Rosi Braidotti writes that "the underlying mood during this pandemic is affective" and "involves complex and internally contradictory alternation of emotions . . . suffering alternating with hope, fear unfolding alongside resilience, boredom merging into vulnerability." From Braidotti's "We are in this together, but we are not one and the same," *Journal of Bioethical Inquiry* 17, no. 4 (2020): 465.

14. "Campeonato Brasileiro de 1937: Saiba como foi o Torneio dos Campeões que o Atlético-MG venceu," *The Lance!* (August 25, 2023). https://www.lance.com.br/atletico-mineiro/campeonato-brasileiro-de-1937-saiba-como-foi-o-torneio-dos-campeoes-que-o-atletico-mg-venceu.html. Accessed August 26, 2023.

15. This was the second Copa do Brasil that Atlético won. In addition to those listed, the club has reached three other continental finals.

16. Tim Vickery reminds us that despite the conspicuous presence within the Brasileirão of several mega clubs, the league has achieved a comparative "competitive balance" since its inception in 1971, especially when compared to leagues in Europe. Vickery, "Unlike Europe, Brazilian league preserves its competitive balance," *SportsIllustrated.com* (May 2, 2010). https://www.si.com/more-sports/2010/05/02/brazil. Accessed January 8, 2021.

17. *Titulares* is the equivalent term for a starting squad in Portuguese.

18. A well-traveled and much-respected coach, Jorge Sampaoli previously led the Chilean national side to its first major trophy by claiming victory in the 2015 Copa América.

19. Fred Ribeiro and Guilherme Frossard, "Jorge Sampaoli Says Goodbye to Atlético-MG," *Globo.com* (February 22, 2021). https://ge.globo.com/futebol/times/atletico-mg/noticia/jorge-sampaoli-se-despede-do-atletico-mg-sigam-caminhando-com-o-coracao-como-guia.ghtml. Accessed May 6, 2022.

20. Pelé's father, João Ramos do Nascimento, nicknamed "Dondinho," was a professional footballer in his own right and played briefly with Atlético Mineiro. Upon the birth of his son in 1940, Dondinho stepped away from Atlético to be with his family and never again suited up for Clube Atlético Mineiro (CAM).

21. The establishment of a professional women's football league in Brazil has made only halting progress in this century, with a three-tiered women's tournament finally gaining a firmer footing in 2013. The "desire" to play that is referenced in this passage is not just generically human, then, but circumstantially gendered and male. The women's side for CAM, which finished as runners-up in the second tier of the competition (Série A2) in 2021, earned promotion with this achievement for the 2022 campaign to the highest echelon of the women's game in Brazil, the Campeonato Brasileiro de Futebol Feminino Série A1.

22. At the 1919 staging, host Brazil claimed the first of its titles in this tournament, the first international football competition to be undertaken in South America when it was launched in 1910. Since 1975, the tournament has been known as the "Copa América." For a historical consideration of the impact of the so-called Spanish flu outbreak on Brazilian football, see Elcio Loureiro Cornelsen, "Futebol em tempos de pandemia, ontem e hoje," *Ludopédio* 129 (March 2020): 1–10.

23. Hamayon, by contrast, describes the "joy" that people experience from their games as "less the expression of spontaneous emotions than the result of a true cultural infusion, which falls within the subject's deepest experience from childhood." From *Why We Play*, 190.

24. These cartels are known as *cartolas* (top hats) in Brazil, as Franklin Foer details in his study *How Soccer Explains the World: An Unlikely Theory of Globalization* (New York: HarperCollins, 2004), 115–140.

25. Roger Kittleson, *The Country of Football: Soccer and the Making of Modern Brazil* (Berkeley: University of California Press, 2014), 5, 9–10. Brazil's movement into modernity has often been described as involving a prolonged conflict between Dionysian play and Apollonian work. For more on the meaning of this conflict in Minas Gerais, see Marcelino Rodrigues da Silva, "A massa faz 100 anos: Futebol e sociedade em BH hoje," *Recorte* 5, no. 2 (2008): 4.

26. Kittleson, *Country of Football*, 49–52.

27. Czech philosopher Vilém Flusser, a longtime resident of Brazil, maintains that the brand of football played by Brazilians is "ontologically" different from that exhibited in the Old World. From Flusser, *Fenomenologia do brasileiro: Em busca de um novo homem*, org. and trans. Gustavo Bernardo (Rio de Janeiro: Editora da Universidade do Estado do Rio de Janeiro, 1998), 100. More broadly, David Goldblatt contends that football constitutes its own reality, however much it might be removed from the pedestrian walks of experience. In Goldblatt's telling, the popular enthusiasm for football "can serve as a collective insistence that there are other moral logics and priorities in this world, different from and more human than the ones we so blithely award the soubriquet of the real." See Goldblatt's *The Age of Football: Soccer and the 21st Century* (New York: Norton, 2020), 3.

28. Sacvan Bercovitch, "The Problem of Ideology in American Literary History," *Critical Inquiry* 12, no. 4 (Summer 1986): 635.

29. Foer, *How Soccer Explains the World*, 1–6.

30. By *feelings*, I refer to a set of emotions that are more visceral and less categorizable than even the provisional "structures of feeling" that Raymond Williams identifies as the always evolving body of popular thought in any period. The feelings that concern me most in this study are thus more personal than the "structural" ones that Williams describes—that is, the feelings that inform this study are actually *felt*. See Williams, *Marxism and Literature* (New York: Oxford University Press, 1977), 128–135.

31. Hans Ulrich Gumbrecht, *In Praise of Athletic Beauty* (Cambridge, MA: Belknap Press of Harvard University Press, 2006), 25–27, 31–33, 54, 86. For an alternative interpretation of "gaming" in the age of COVID-19, refer to Wai Chee Dimock, "Gaming the Pandemic," *PMLA* 136, no. 2 (March 2021): 163–170.

32. See the Galo website maintained by Atlético fan and Tulane University professor Idelber Avelar, http://www.tulane.edu/~avelar/galo.html. Accessed January 6, 2021.

33. Vicente Mota is from Montes Claros, a city located in the north of Minas Gerais state.

34. "Brazil Scrambles to Approve Coronavirus Vaccine as Pressure Mounts," *Los Angeles Times* (January 1, 2021). https://www.latimes.com/world-nation/story/2021-01-01/brazil-scrambles-to-approve-virus-vaccine-as-pressure-mounts. Accessed January 6, 2021.

35. According to Ian Frazier, "America construes itself as a game that anybody can play." From Frazier's "Rereading 'Lolita,'" *The New Yorker* (December 14, 2020): 35. As for the uneven formation of Brazil's own national political culture, David Goldblatt emphasizes the role that has been assumed in that country by the "collective ritual" of football, which has helped bind together a pluralistic nation of vast geographic proportions. See Goldblatt's *Futebol Nation: A Footballing History of Brazil* (London: Penguin, 2014), xviii–xix.

36. The recent work of social psychologists figures an exception in this regard, as scientists attempt to measure the role that team sports plays in personal emotional development. See, for example, Mickael Campo, Diane M. Mackie, and Xavier Sanchez, "Emotions in Group Sports: A Narrative Review from a Social Identity Perspective," *Frontiers in Psychology* 10 (2019): 666–682.

37. Eduardo Galeano, *Soccer in Sun and Shadow* (1995; rept. New York: Verso, 1999), 3.

38. Ricardo Galuppo, *Raça e amor: A saga do Clube Atlético Mineiro vista da arquibancada* (São Paulo: DBA Editora, 2005), 190, 196.

39. Ibid., 194. The fan whom Galuppo cites self-identifies as Kalil Baracat Filho, "Kalil" being the surname of the Brazilian family who produced not one but two past presidents of CAM. Elias Kalil served as the administrative head of Atlético from 1980 to 1985, while his son Alexandre served in this same capacity between 2008 and 2014 before taking office as the mayor of Belo Horizonte in 2017.

40. For a monthly fee, the holders of this card receive several baseline benefits, including one official Atlético Mineiro jersey per season, first priority for ordering ticket packages and single tickets to CAM matches, and discounts for any purchases of said packages. Additional benefits accrue to those who pay into a higher level of monthly fees within this three-tiered promotions program. As of May 12, 2022, the Galo Na Veia plan had

132,963 subscribers. See https://galonaveia.atletico.com.br/home. Accessed May 31, 2022.

41. More studies are needed regarding the diminishing emotional commitments that players can often demonstrate for their "first" clubs after they make repeated professional moves between different sides. For treatment of this phenomenon in Brazil, see Fábio Padilha Alves, "Amor à camisa? Conciliando razão e paixão no ambiente do futebol professional" (Dissertações de mestrado, Programa de Pós-Graduação em Educação Física, Universidade Federal do Espírito Santo, 2010), 63–71.

42. Galuppo, *Raça e amor*, 45–46, 56.

43. Diego Garcia, Marcus Alves, and Rafael Valente, "Dos grandes, só Palmeiras não aderiu ao parcelamento de dívida com a união," *ESPN.com.br* (November 25, 2015). http://www.espn.com.br/noticia/560080_dos -grandes-so-palmeiras-nao-aderiu-ao-parcelamento-de-divida-com-a-uniao. Accessed May 15, 2022.

44. Dan Horch, "Brazilian Soccer's Financial Disarray Starts to Show on the Field," *New York Times* (April 23, 2015). https://www.nytimes .com/2015/04/24/sports/soccer/brazilian-soccers-financial-disarray-starts-to -show-on-the-field.html. Accessed May 15, 2022.

45. Galuppo, *Raça e amor*, 114; and "City Football Group Bid for Atlético Mineiro," *Reuters* (March 22, 2022). https://www.reuters.com/markets /funds/city-football-group-bid-atletico-mineiro-report-2022-03-07/. Accessed May 14, 2022.

46. CAM's debt for 2019, confirmed by *Estado de Minas* to be around R$746 million (approximately US$137.8 million), marked an increase of R$300 million (approximately US$55.4 million) from the previous year. CAM does not officially make its financial figures public, but this disproportionate increase in borrowing was attributed at the time to the effects of the coronavirus pandemic. From Fred Ribeiro, "Without Forecasting to Vote on 2020 Balance Sheet, Atlético-MG Prepares Event to Show Financial Reality; Debt Exceeds R$1 Billion," *Globo.com* (March 26, 2021). https://globoesporte.globo.com/futebol/times/atletico-mg/noticia /sem-previsao-em-votar-balanco-de-2020-atletico-mg-prepara-evento-para -mostrar-realidade-financeira-divida-ultrapassa-r-1-bilhao.ghtml. Accessed March 26, 2021.

47. Ana Tur-Porcar and Domingo Ribeiro-Soriano, "The Role of Emotions and Motivations in Sports Organizations," *Frontiers in Psychology* 11 (October 2020), 12–19. Special issue on "The Management of Emotions in Sports Organizations," ed. Manuel Alonso Dos Santos, Ferran Calabuig Moreno, and Irena Valantine.

48. Sianne Ngai, *Ugly Feelings* (Cambridge, MA: Harvard University Press, 2005), 1–37.

49. Galuppo, *Raça e amor*, 72.
50. Ibid., 147, 149. Reinaldo began playing as a member of Atlético's first-team squad at the early age of seventeen.
51. Ibid., 147.
52. Ibid., 154.
53. Ibid., 24.
54. Among the founders of this virtual syndicate are Clube Atlético Mineiro, Cruzeiro Esporte Clube, Sport Club Corinthians Paulista, Santos Futebol Clube, São Paulo Futebol Clube, Sociedade Esportiva Palmeiras, Botafogo de Futebol e Regatas, Clube de Regatas do Flamengo, Fluminense Football Club, Club de Regatas Vasco da Gama, Grêmio de Futebol Porto Alegre, Sport Club Internacional, and Esporte Clube Bahia. The "treze" clubs of the original union were later expanded, thereby increasing the leverage of the members as they negotiated the broadcast rights for matches. For more on the comparative performances of member clubs in recent years, see Elcio Loureiro Cornelsen, "Protagonistas e coadjuvantes—Um olhar para o desempenho de clubes no Campeonato Brasileiro da Série A (2010–2019)," *Ludopédio* 114 (May 17, 2021): 1–12.
55. Franklin Velasco and Rafael Jorda, "Portrait of Boredom among Athletes and Its Implications in Sports Management: A Multi-Method Approach," *Frontiers in Psychology* 11 (October 2020), 29–40. Special issue on "The Management of Emotions in Sports Organizations," ed. Manuel Alonso Dos Santos, Ferran Calabuig Moreno, and Irena Valantine.
56. Galuppo, *Raça e amor*, 173.
57. Walt Whitman, *Leaves of Grass* (Brooklyn, New York, 1855), 15. Whitman, of course, was born in a time and place that precluded the possibility of his knowing the game that Americans would come to recognize as "soccer." He was an early enthusiast of the game of baseball, however, and wrote in the *Brooklyn Daily Eagle* for July 23, 1846, "The game of ball is glorious." For more on Whitman's interest in the latter sport, see John Thorn, "Whitman, Melville, and Baseball: Some Bicentennial Musings," *mlblogs.com* (June 15, 2012). https://ourgame.mlblogs.com/whitman-melville-and-baseball-662f5ef3583d. Accessed June 20, 2022.
58. On the "modern" rivalry between CAM and Cruzeiro, see Marcelino Rodrigues da Silva, "A cidade dividida nas charges de Mangabeira," *Revista Z* 6 (2010). https://revistazcultural-pacc-ufrj-br.translate.goog/a-cidade-dividida-nas-charges-de-mangabeira-de-marcelino-rodrigues-da-silva/?_x_tr_sch=http&_x_tr_sl=pt&_x_tr_tl=en&_x_tr_hl=en&_x_tr_pto=sc. Accessed May 23, 2022.
59. Loureiro Cornelsen, "Protagonistas e coadjuvantes," 1–12.
60. Doris Bergen, "Psychological Approaches to the Study of Play," *American Journal of Play* 7, no. 3 (Fall 2015): 104.

Chapter 2

1. In the original Portuguese from this Brazilian classic, the line from my epigraph for this chapter reads, "Lembra-vos ainda a minha teoria das edições humanas?"

2. Interview with Nelinho. Sion—Belo Horizonte, Brazil. May 30, 2022. In addition to playing for Clube Atlético Mineiro (CAM), Nelinho also managed Atlético Mineiro during the 1993 campaign, long enough for him to realize that coaching, as he said, was "not for [him]."

3. Ibid.

4. Ibid. Sitting in on my conversation with Nelinho was his youngest daughter, who reminded her father that although he might have twin loyalties to Cruzeiro and Atlético Mineiro, his three daughters and grandchildren do not. The former are unabashed *atleticanas*, the latter *atleticanos*.

5. Interview with Bolivar. Lisbon, Portugal (Zoom). June 3, 2022. Bolivar worked for the *Alterosa esporte* program from 2005 to 2008 and then again from 2011 to 2014.

6. Ibid.

7. Ibid.

8. Roberto DaMatta, "Sport in Society: An Essay on Brazilian Football," *VIBRANT* 6, no. 2 (December 2009): 103–104. Original emphasis.

9. Gregory E. Jackson, "*Malandros*: 'Honourable Workers' and the Professionalization of Brazilian Football, 1930–1950," in *The Country of Football: Politics, Popular Culture, and the Beautiful Game in Brazil*, ed. Paulo Fontes and Bernardo Borges Buarque de Hollanda (London: Hurst, 2014), 43–44.

10. Edgard Cornacchione and Liliane Klaus, "Ethical Business Culture in Brazil: Advantages and Obstacles of National Jeitinho," in *Ethical Business Cultures in Emerging Markets*, ed. Douglas Jondle and Alexandre Ardichvili (New York: Cambridge University Press, 2017), 9–10, 13–14.

11. Created in 2003 under former (and current) President Luiz Inácio Lula da Silva, or "Lula," Bolsa Família continues to divide opinion in Brazil. For a discussion of this program's reception in Minas Gerais, see "The Bolsa Família Program," in *The Brazil Reader: History, Culture, Politics*, ed. James N. Green, Victoria Langland, and Lilia Moritz Schwarcz (Durham: Duke University Press, 2019), 523–525.

12. Cornacchione and Klaus, "Ethical Business Culture in Brazil," 15–16.

13. Frantz Fanon, *Black Skin, White Masks*, trans. Charles Lam Markmann (1952; rept. New York: Grove Press, 1967), 10.

14. Stuart Hall, "Race, the Floating Signifier: What More Is There to Say about 'Race'?," in *Selected Writings on Race and Difference*, ed. Paul Gilroy and Ruth Wilson Gilmore (Durham: Duke University Press, 2021), 359–360, 362, 371.

15. Ben Carrington, *Race, Sport and Politics: The Sporting Black Diaspora* (London: SAGE, 2010), 3–4, 45–46. Original emphasis.
16. Filipe Fernandes Ribeiro Mostaro, Ronaldo George Helal, and Fausto Amaro, "Futebol, nação e representações: A importância do estilo 'futebol-arte' na construção da identidade nacional," *História Unisinos* 19, no. 3 (2015): 272–282; and Ronaldo Helal and Cesar Gordon Jr., "Sociologia, história e romance na construção da indentidade nacional através do futebol," in Ronaldo Helal, Antônio Jorge Soares, and Hugo Lovisolo, *A invenção do país do futebol: Mídia, raça e idolatria* (Rio de Janeiro: Mauad, 2012), 67–69.
17. Gilberto Freyre, "Foot-ball mulatto," *Diário de Pernambuco* (June 17, 1938): 4. In this century, David Goldblatt has similarly spoken of Brazilian *futebol* as what he calls a "game of flow rather than sequence," and on this basis, he speaks to "the deep ludic basis of football's popularity" in the country. From Goldblatt, *The Age of Football*, 464–465.
18. "A vez do preto" is the title of the sixth and final chapter of Mário Filho's book, *O negro no futebol Brasileiro*, a revised and expanded edition of which he brought forth in 1964. See *O negro no futebol Brasileiro* (1947; rept. Rio de Janeiro: Mauad X, 2010), 285–293.
19. Tiago Fernandes Maranhão and Jorge Knijnik, "Futebol Mulato: Racial Constructs in Brazilian Football," *Cosmopolitan Civil Societies Journal* 3, no. 2 (2011): 57–58. Antonio Soares reminds us that any discussion of racism in modern Brazil must find a way to balance universalist with regional claims while also accounting for the peculiar dynamics of football's social significance in the country. From Soares, "Futebol, raça e nacionalidade no Brasil: Releitura da história official" (Doutorado em Educação Fisica, Universidade Gama Filho, Rio de Janeiro, 1998), 11.
20. Fernandes Maranhão and Knijnik, "Futebol Mulato," 58–59, 60.
21. The former Flamengo defender Juvenal Amarijo also came under criticism in the press for the defeat, but many Brazilians attributed the loss to Brazilian goalkeeper Moacir Barbosa, who would shoulder the burden for the defeat until his death in 2000. The negative outcome of the match, more generally, weighs heavily in Brazil and is remembered to this day as *Maracanazo*, or "the Maracanã blow," Maracanã being the stadium in Rio de Janeiro where the defeat occurred.
22. Brazilian journalist Milly Lacombe was instrumental in garnering attention for Sueli Carneiro's interview. She used her position as a well-known sports columnist for *UOL* to endorse Carneiro's claim in the online journal's May 28, 2022, issue. Additional media outlets subsequently ran Lacombe's story, causing no small controversy in Brazil. See Lacombe, "The Whitening of Brazilian Football According to the Philosopher Sueli Carneiro," *UOL* (May 28, 2022). https://www.uol.com.br/esporte/colunas/milly-lacombe/2022/05/28/mano-brown-e-sueli-carneiro-o-embranquecimento-do-futebol-brasileiro.htm. Accessed June 9, 2022.

23. Grant Farred, *Only a Black Athlete Can Save Us Now* (Minneapolis: University of Minnesota Press, 2022).

24. "Os Brasileiros campeões Sul-Americanos de remo," *Jornal dos Sports* (March 23, 1931): 1. Among the paper's principal owners was the writer Mário Filho, whose book *O negro no futebol Brasileiro* is discussed earlier.

25. The first instance within the paper of *raça* being used in a footballing sense occurred on March 28, 1931, in the article "O Fluminense em grande forma." Here, two of the Rio de Janeiro side Fluminense's *white* footballers, the Italianate Demosthenes and Amaury, were presented to readers as "*dois rapazes* [young men] *de raça.*" From *Jornal dos Sports* (March 28, 1931): 1, 4. Not long afterward, the goalkeeper for the Brazilian club Andarahy, Walter de Souza Goulart, or "Walter" for short, was also announced as "*Um keeper de raça*" in an article carrying that same headline from April 18, 1931, p. 2. The same year, French boxer Guy Bonaugure was referred to as "*um boxeur de raça,*" before subsequent discussion of boxing in the months to follow made mention of a "*raça Latina*" and a "*raça Negra.*" In the last case, the Black athlete in question was Canadian boxer George Godfrey, known by the sporting press as "Old Chocolate" late in his career and represented here as "*um gigantesco negro.*" See the following articles, respectively, from *Jornal dos Sports*: "Os melhores pugilistas Francezes" (May 12, 1931): 4; "Os gigantes no pugilismo" (May 20, 1931): 4; and "Combates de gigantes" (August 28, 1931): 3.

26. "Rio é carnaval," *Jornal dos Sports* (January 16, 1968): 7. A veteran of three World Cups (1954, 1958, and 1962) for Brazil, Waldyr Pereira, or "Didi," is widely considered to be one of the best footballers of all time.

27. "Vasco usa tôda raça para impor a técnica," *Jornal dos Sports* (February 12, 1968): 3.

28. The previously mentioned Fluminense was one such team. Eking out a goalless away draw at Paissandu Atlético Clube, better known as "Paissandu," Fluminense was commended for demonstrating *raça* despite being otherwise outmatched on the day. "Flu aplica raça para empatar em Belém," *Jornal dos Sports* (February 10, 1968): 3.

29. "Quem tem mêdo do nôvo Vasco da Gama?," *Jornal dos Sports* (April 2, 1968): 5.

30. Thomas E. Skidmore, "Race and Class in Brazil: Historical Perspectives," *Luso-Brazilian Review* 20, no. 1 (Summer 1983): 104–118.

31. Marilene Dabus, "Negros podem ser brancos," *Jornal dos Sports* (July 23, 1971): 4. Dabus frames her interview with a short report on a recent meeting of the American Medical Association, at which a U.S. physician related that during the Second World War, it was discovered that the application of certain chemicals to the skin of some Black workers who were employed in the leather industry had turned their skin "white."

The more immediate inspiration for Dabus's article, however, would have been the notorious case of the Brazilian right back Carlos Alberto Torres. "*O Capitão do Tri*," as he became known, was the first Black player to represent Fluminense, a club that was founded by upper-class whites in Rio de Janeiro in 1902. Such was the pressure experienced by Carlos Alberto during his first years with the club, from 1963 to 1966, that he sometimes took to whitening his face with rice powder before matches. For more on Carlos Alberto's trials of racial representation, see Alex Bellos, *Futebol: The Brazilian Way of Life* (New York: Bloomsbury, 2002), 32.

32. Kittleson, *Country of Football*, 126. For a more recent examination by Kittleson of what he calls "mulatto football," see his profile of 1930s Brazilian player Fausto dos Santos, who became known after his fine performance at the 1930 World Cup as "*Maravilha Negra*," or "Black Wonder." From Roger Kittleson, "Fausto dos Santos: The Wonders and Challenges of Blackness in Brazil's 'Mulatto Football,'" in *Football and the Boundaries of History: Critical Studies in Soccer*, ed. Brenda Elsey and Stanislao G. Pugliese (New York: Palgrave Macmillan, 2017), 161–178.

33. Philipe Van R. Lima, *Punho cerrado: A história do rei* (Belo Horizonte: Letramento, 2017), 42.

34. "Confidencial," *Jornal dos Sports* (April 2, 1977): 2.

35. Interview with Reinaldo. Palácio das Mangabeiras—Belo Horizonte, Brazil. June 3, 2022.

36. Cristiano Martins, "Risco de morte por Covid é 46% maior entre a população negra em Minas Gerais," *Otempo* (July 10, 2020). https://www.otemp.com.br/cidades/risco-de-morte-por-covid-e-46-maior-entre-a-populacao-negra-em-minas-gerais-1.2358721. Accessed June 8, 2022.

37. Interview with Reinaldo.

38. Vicente Mota borrowed some of the lyrics and melody for CAM's anthem from Flamengo, a club that is based in Rio de Janeiro, where samba carries a wider cultural appeal than it does in Belo Horizonte. See Marcelino Rodrigues da Silva, "Quem não gosta de samba . . . não é doente do pé: Carnaval e futebol em Belo Horizonte," *Revista Interfaces* 11 (2008): 86–87; and Elcio Cornelsen and Erilma Desiree da Silva, "A trilha sonora dos times das gerais," *Suplemento: O Futebol no Campo das Letras* (June 2014): 28–29.

39. Bernardo Buarque de Hollanda describes "two dimensions" to the organized supporters' groups in Brazil for the period 1950–1980, when the crowd culture that we find in the country's football stadiums today was taking shape. One of these cultures he names "the disciplinary," the other "the festive." From Hollanda, "The Competitive Party: The Formation and Crisis of Organized Fan Groups in Brazil, 1950–1980," in *Football and the Boundaries of History: Critical Studies in Soccer*, ed. Brenda Elsey and Stanislao G. Pugliese (New York: Palgrave Macmillan, 2017), 296.

40. Interview with Reinaldo. Also see Galo's "Yes We C.A.M." video, which can be found at https://www.youtube.com/watch?v=1tzlJUa1zNM. Accessed May 8, 2022. The slogan "Yes We C.A.M.," of course, refers to President Barack Obama's "Yes We Can" campaign rallying call from 2008, which is also the source for an additional motto that Galo improvised during the 2013 Copa Libertadores run, *Eu Acredito* (I Believe).

41. David Goldblatt observes that attendance levels at domestic football matches in Brazil have declined sharply since the country hosted the World Cup in 2014. Part of this decline may be attributed to the price of tickets the Brasileirão charges. Relative to real wages, these tickets are among the highest in the world. From Goldblatt, *Age of Football*, 178–179.

42. Interview with Reinaldo.

43. "Turco Says It's Difficult to Explain Atlético-MG's Defeat to Flumi-nense," *Goa Spotlight* (June 2022). https://thegoaspotlight.com/2022/06/09 /turco-says-its-difficult-to-explain-atletico-mgs-defeat-to-fluminense-night -to-forget-athletic-mg/. Accessed June 13, 2022.

44. Machado de Assis, *Memorías póstumas de Brás Cubas* (1880; rept. São Paulo: Ateliê Editorial, 2004), 131. In the newspaper chronicles that he composed for the press in the city of Rio de Janeiro in the late nineteenth century, Machado de Assis applied his usual ironic perspective to the cultural phenomenon of sport, which phenomenon he otherwise regarded as having historical importance for Brazil. For more on the author's artistic relationship to sport, see Victor Melo, "Olhares irônicos: Machado de Assis e o esporte," *Aletria* 26, no. 3 (2016): 123–140.

45. Bernd Bucher and Julian Eck, "Football's Contribution to International Order: The Ludic and Festive Reproduction of International Society by World Societal Actors," *International Theory* (2021): 14, 22.

46. After securing a 2–2 draw away to Tijuana in the first leg of the quarterfinal tie, Atlético secured its famous passage through to the semi-finals after CAM's former goalkeeper, Victor, saved a penalty in a match that has since come to be known as the "*Milagre do Horto*." Due to reno-vations at the Mineirão, this "miracle" of a match was played at the Está-dio Independência of América-MG in the "Horto" neighborhood of Belo Horizonte. For more on this encounter, see *O milagre do horto*, ed. André Fidusi, Fernando Gregori, and Frederico Jota (São Paulo: Coletivo Editorial, 2016). Mexican clubs stopped competing in the Copa Libertadores in 2017, although discussions are ongoing for their return. Teams from what is now known as Liga MX compete with other club teams from the Caribbean and North and Central America in the regionally constituted CONCACAF Champions League.

47. Matt Schudel, "Dom Phillips, Journalist Who Chronicled Amazon Deforestation, Is Dead at 57," *Washington Post* (June 18, 2022). https:// www.washingtonpost.com/obituaries/2022/06/17/dom-phillips-brazil-dies/.

Accessed June 19, 2022. Writing for the newspaper *Folha de São Paulo*, Phillips commemorated CAM's first Copa Libertadores title in 2013 by explaining the meaning of the side's catchphrase *"Eu Acredito"* (I Believe) to an English-speaking audience. Phillips's article, "Atlético Take Libertadores—Finally," can be read in its entirety in the *Folha de São Paulo* for July 25, 2013, at https://www1.folha.uol.com.br/mundo/2013/07/1316852-from-brazil-atletico-take-libertadores—-finally.shtml. Accessed June 22, 2022.

48. Fred Melo Paiva, "Contra o Flamengo, grileiro dos nossos sonhos, a guerra," *Jornal Estado de Minas* (June 18, 2022). https://www.em.com.br/app/colunistas/fred-melo-paiva/2022/06/18/interna_fred_melo_paiva,1374116/contra-o-flamengo-grileiro-dos-nossos-sonhos-a-guerra.shtml. Accessed June 19, 2022.

49. Stephanie Burnett, "Mick Jagger Is Being Blamed for Brazil's World Cup Thrashing," *Time* (July 9, 2014). https://time.com/2968373/world-cup-brazil-mick-jagger-football-soccer/. Accessed June 19, 2022.

50. "Atlético-MG mantém escrita sobre o Flamengo em Minas," *The Lance!* (June 19, 2022). https://www.lance.com.br/atletico-mineiro/atletico-mg-mantem-escrita-sobre-o-flamengo-em-minas-e-turco-mohamed-ganha-folego-com-vitoria.html. Accessed June 20, 2022.

51. The reference is to a famous line from Gertrude Stein's 1913 poem "Sacred Emily," which appears in her book *Geography and Plays* (1922). The original line reads, "Rose is a rose is a rose is a rose." Yet the author employs variants in wording at later stages in her career, notably with the article "A" preceding the line. See Stein's *Geography and Plays*, ed. Cyrena N. Pondrom (Madison: University of Wisconsin Press, 1993), 187. For more on the "semiotic play" of Stein's work, see Charles Bernstein, "Gertrude Stein," *A History of Modernist Poetry*, ed. Alex Davis and Lee M. Jenkins (New York: Cambridge University Press, 2015), 263.

52. Interview with João Leite. Assembleia Legislativa de Minas Gerais—Belo Horizonte, Brazil. August 10, 2022.

53. João Leite da Silva Neto, *João Leite: O goleiro de deus em preto e branco* (Belo Horizonte: 2019), 63.

54. Both players, one active and the other retired, were staunch supporters of former Brazilian president Jair Bolsonaro.

55. Marcus Alves, "Evangelicalism and Brazil: The Religious Movement That Spread through a National Team," *BBC Sport* (March 22, 2022). https://www.bbc.com/sport/football/60483820. Accessed August 13, 2022.

56. Interview with João Leite. We need not wonder whether Leite has passed down *futebol* within his own family: His son, Helton Leite, was the former goalkeeper at renowned Portuguese side Benfica before playing for Antalyaspor in the Turkish Süper Lig.

57. Gabriela Alcantara Azevedo Cavalcanti de Arruda, Daniel Medeiros de Freitas, Carolina Maria Soares Lima, Krzysztof Nawratek, and Ber-

nardo Miranda Pataro, "The Production of Knowledge through Religious and Social Media Infrastructure: World Making Practices among Brazilian Pentecostals," *Popular Communication* (May 4, 2022): 5.

58. Interview with Rafael Miranda. Belo Horizonte, Brazil (Zoom). August 12, 2022.

59. Ibid.

60. Ibid.

61. Kenneth Burke, "Literature as Equipment for Living," *The Philosophy of Literary Form: Studies in Symbolic Action* (Baton Rouge: Louisiana State University Press, 1941), 292–304.

62. Interview with Réver. Belo Horizonte, Brazil (WhatsApp chat). June 27, 2022.

63. Ibid.

64. Interview with Victor. Belo Horizonte, Brazil (WhatsApp chat). August 24, 2022.

65. Interview with Réver.

66. Ibid.

67. Ibid.

68. Ibid. Réver's agent, Gustavo Faria, explained the circumstances behind his client's withdrawal from the match against Athletico Paranaense in a WhatsApp chat from August 9, 2022.

Chapter 3

1. Mark Holowchak, "Freud on Play, Games, and Sports Fanaticism," *Journal of the American Academy of Psychoanalysis and Dynamic Psychiatry* 39, no. 4 (2011): 696.

2. Ibid., 707–708.

3. The quote comes from the father of the novel's probable protagonist, Florentino Ariza, and it is a sentiment that the former character expresses in his private notebook some time before the birth of his son. See Gabriel García Márquez, *Love in the Time of Cholera*, trans. Edith Grossman (1985; rept. New York: Penguin, 1989), 169. In an earlier short story, "El juramento" (1983), the native Colombian author García Márquez makes his one overt foray into football writing by arranging for the narrator of his tale to attend a hotly contested match between Barranquilla-based Atletico Junior and the Bogotá side Millionarios. With "El juramento" (The Oath), moreover, García Márquez deploys the same metaphor that I am using in *That Futebol Feeling*—that is, the fever for football being not unlike an infection that spreads.

4. If Freud has nothing to say about football, then Brazilian playwright, journalist, and novelist Nelson Rodrigues has little more than a nominal interest in Freud, the title of his essay "Freud no futebol" (1956)

notwithstanding. Although the writer might not have cared to thread the needle of Freud's love and death drives, he does express a sentiment in his essay that Freud might have endorsed. Surveying the sports world that he occupied in Rio de Janeiro in the 1950s, Rodrigues writes, "No one remembers to preserve inner health, the delicate emotional balance of the player," whose condition our writer describes as one of "excruciating psychic fragility" (29). And because of this emotional vulnerability, Rodrigues concludes, we find that "the Brazilian player is always . . . in crisis" (30). See Rodrigues, "Freud no futebol," in *À sombra das chuteiras imortais: Crônicas de futebol*, ed. Ruy Castro (São Paulo: Companhia das Letra, 1993), 29–31. Pertinent to the themes of this chapter, Rodrigues also wrote multiple stories and novels that treat love thematically, often for a primary audience of female readers. Among the stories that fit this description are Rodrigues's resonantly titled "A história de amor," which appeared on page 2 of the Sunday morning edition of Rio de Janeiro's *Globo* newspaper on June 10, 1973.

5. Felipe Tavares Paes Lopes and Mariana Prioli Cordeiro, "Futebol, massa e poder: Reflexões sobre a 'teoria do contágio,'" *Psicologia Política* 15, no. 34 (2015): 481–482.

6. *Lutar, lutar, lutar* (2021), dir. Sérgio Borges and Helvécio Marins Jr.

7. Interview with Helvécio Marins Jr. Lisbon, Portugal (Zoom). June 28, 2022.

8. Ibid. Marins pointed out that all his Clube idols (including Reinaldo, Ronaldinho, and Jo) are Black players, and not by coincidence. As we have seen, Clube Atlético Mineiro (CAM) was one of the first Brazilian clubs, along with the Rio de Janeiro side Vasco da Gama, to field Black players. The filmmaker also claimed that CAM's Black players have always been the team's most reliable exemplars of the *raça* that is *amor*'s necessary corollary.

9. Interview with Alice Quintão Soares. Salvador, Brazil (Zoom). June 27, 2022.

10. Ibid.

11. Eric Lott, *Love and Theft: Blackface Minstrelsy and the American Working Class* (New York: Oxford University Press, 1993), 39–65.

12. Interview with Alice Quintão Soares.

13. Brenda Elsey and Joshua Nadel, *Futbolera: A History of Women and Sports in Latin America* (Austin: University of Texas Press, 2019), 61–63.

14. The Milan Court of Appeals upheld Robinho's nine-year prison sentence in 2020, as did the highest court in Italy in January 2022. At the time of my writing, the accused has not yet served any portion of his term. See Adriana Garcia, "Milan Court: Robinho 'Brutally Humiliated' Victim," *ESPN.com* (March 10, 2021). https://www.espn.com/soccer/acmi

lan/story/4334518/milan-court-robinho-brutally-humiliated-rape-victim. Accessed July 24, 2023.

15. Luisa Turbino Torres, "The Politics of Being a Soccer Fan: An Ethnographic Perspective on Feminist Activism around Soccer in Brazil" (Ph.D. Dissertation, Political Science and International Relations, University of Delaware, 2022), 5.

16. Bruno Carvalho, "O que se sabe sobre o caso envolvendo Cuca na Suíça," *UOL* (March 3, 2021). https://www.uol.com.br/esporte/futebol /ultimas-noticias/2021/03/03/o-que-se-sabe-sobre-o-caso-envolvendo-cuca -na-suica-em-1987.htm. Accessed June 24, 2023.

17. Tom Phillips, "'Lack of Shame': Robinho Scandal Highlights Brazil's Rape Crisis," *The Guardian* (October 22, 2020). https://www.the guardian.com/world/2020/oct/22/brazil-rape-robinho-santos. Accessed July 18, 2023.

18. Torres, "Politics of Being a Soccer Fan," 5–6.

19. Interview with Helvécio Marins Jr.

20. André Martins, "A positividade das alegrias partilhadas: Reflexões filosóficas sobre o arrebatamento pelo futebol como afirmação da vida, de nossa própria potência e da potência do coletivo," in *Uma bola no pé uma ideia na cabeça: O que o futebol nos faz pensar*, ed. Arthur L. F. Ferreira, André Martins, and Robert Segal (Rio de Janeiro: Editora Universidade Federal do Rio de Janeiro, 2014), 483.

21. Túlio Mayã Ferreira Barros de Souza, "Relação entre estresse e ansiedade no rendimento de atletas de futebol de campo" (Bacharel em Educação Física, Universidade Federal de Pernambuco, Centro Acadêmico de Vitória, 2019), 16.

22. To decide the winner in the opening round of group play for a bracket that included both clubs, Flamengo faced off against CAM in a specially arranged match held at the Serra Dourada Stadium in Goiânia on August 21 for the right to advance to the next round of the Copa Libertadores. After no fewer than five Atlético players were sent off in the opening minutes of the match, leaving the team unable to field a competitive side, the game was called in Flamengo's favor at 0–0 in the thirty-seventh minute.

23. *Lutar, lutar, lutar.*

24. Felipe Alexandre de Souza Félix Nunes and Jonathan Simões Freitas, "Combination of Factors for the Presence of the Public: A Look at the Lower Levels of Football in Minas Gerais," *Revista Intercontinental de Gestão* 11 (2021): 1–3, 8–9.

25. *Lutar, lutar, lutar.*

26. Ibid.

27. Hilde Hein, "Play as an Aesthetic Concept," *Journal of Aesthetics and Art Criticism* 27, no. 1 (Autumn 1968): 67. For eighteenth-century German playwright, poet, and philosopher Friedrich Schiller, the "play

impulse" is a human condition that combines thinking with feeling, "contingency with necessity," and "passivity with freedom" (XV: 62–63). Schiller contends, in his own words, that "it is precisely play, and play alone, that makes man complete and displays at once his twofold nature" (XV: 64). From Schiller, *Letters on the Aesthetic Education of Man*, trans. Reginald Snell (1794; rept. Mineola, NY: Dover Publications, 2004).

28. Interview with Fred Melo Paiva. Caraíva, Brazil (Zoom). July 8, 2022.

29. Fred Melo Paiva, "Uma chance para o acerto de contas do Galo com o Flamengo," *Jornal Estado de Minas* (July 9, 2022). https://www .em.com.br/app/colunistas/fred-melo-paiva/2022/07/09/interna_fred _melo_paiva,1378991/uma-chance-para-o-acerto-de-contas-do-galo-com -o-flamengo.shtml. Accessed July 9, 2022.

30. Interview with Fred Melo Paiva. Also see the "timeless and utopian dimension" of football that José Miguel Wisnik attests to in *Veneno remédio: O futebol e o Brasil* (São Paulo: Companhia das Letras, 2008), 31. For Wisnik, football represents "time without time" (190).

31. Wisnik, *Veneno remédio*, 60; and Hilário Franco Júnior, "Ensaio bibliográfico," *Revista de História* 163 (July–December 2010): 379.

32. Interview with Fred Melo Paiva; and Paiva, "Uma chance para o acerto de contas do Galo com o Flamengo."

33. Interview with Fred Melo Paiva.

34. Ibid.

35. WhatsApp chat with Frederico Bolivar, July 9, 2022.

36. Interview with Rodolfo Gropen. Savassi—Belo Horizonte, Brazil. July 12, 2022.

37. Fred Ribeiro, "De torcedor a 'homem forte' do Atlético: O choro dos filhos que mudou a vida de Rodolfo Gropen," *Hoje em Dia* (November 11, 2021). https://www.hojeemdia.com.br/esportes/de-torcedor-a-homem -forte-do-atletico-o-choro-dos-filhos-que-mudou-a-vida-de-rodolfo-gro pen-1.425161. Accessed July 8, 2022.

38. Ibid.

39. Interview with Rodolfo Gropen.

40. Ibid.

41. Ibid. The article "*o*" (the) signifies for Gropen that Atlético is the club of "*the* people" (emphasis Gropen's).

42. Carol Leandro's original words were "O Galo não jogou nada!" ("Galo didn't play at all!"). See "Eliminado, Atlético-MG deixa escapar prêmio milionário e fecha a Copa do Brasil com R$4,9 milhões," *Globo. com* (July 14, 2022). https://ge.globo.com/futebol/times/atletico-mg/not icia/2022/07/14/eliminado-atletico-mg-deixa-escapar-premio-milionario -e-fecha-a-copa-do-brasil-com-r-49-milhoes.ghtml. Accessed July 16, 2022.

43. WhatsApp chat with Rodolfo Gropen, July 14, 2022.

44. "Eliminado."

45. The most famous version of these words in world sports was spoken (and subsequently misquoted) in May 1981 by Scotsman Bill Shankly, longtime manager for England's Liverpool FC. In discussing his devotion to the game with Granada TV, Shankly expressed a sentiment to the following effect: "Some people believe football is a matter of life and death; I am very disappointed with that attitude. I can assure you it is much, much more important than that." See Mark Jones, "Bill Shankly's Famous 'Life and Death' Misquote and What Liverpool Icon Really Meant," *Mirror* (March 31, 2020). https://www.mirror.co.uk/sport/football/news/bill-shanklys-famous-life-death-21784583. Accessed July 16, 2022.

46. Interview with Carol Leandro. Belo Horizonte, Brazil (Zoom). July 20, 2022.

47. Leandro at one stage learned to speak Spanish, only to discover that the language lacks a proper way to convey the meaning of *raça*. She improvised with the Spanish phrase *poner gana* (to get wins) before deciding in time that this expression was insufficient. From Ibid.

48. Ibid.

49. For more on what the authors describe as "the distinction between reference and referent" in Brazil's footballing discourse, see Chantal Duarte Silva and Gustavo Miranda Guimarães, "The Constitution of Brazilian Footballing Speech Objects: Atlético Mineiro Club as a Club of Great Achievements or a Discursive Object Well Built?," *International Journal of Language and Linguistics* 3, no. 5 (November 2016): 84.

50. Interview with Carol Leandro.

51. Ibid.

52. Interview with Márcio de Lima Leite. Casa Fiat de Cultura—Belo Horizonte, Brazil. July 21, 2022.

53. Ibid. Formed in 2021 after a fifty-fifty merger between the Italian American conglomerate Fiat Chrysler Automobiles and the French PSA Group, Stellantis N.V. is a multinational automotive manufacturing corporation headquartered in Amsterdam.

54. Nunes and Freitas, "Combination of Factors for the Presence of the Public," 2.

55. Interview with Márcio de Lima Leite.

56. Ibid.

57. Carlos Etiene de Castro, "Moura Costa," *Jornal Estado de Minas* (April 2, 1950): 4.

58. Drawing from *Great Brazilian Clubs Magazine*, *Galo Digital* provides a more complete portrait of Costa than is offered here. See https://www-galodigital-com-br.translate.goog/enciclopedia/Leandro_Castilho_Moura_Costa?_x_tr_sch=http&_x_tr_sl=pt&_x_tr_tl=en&_x_tr_hl=en&_x_tr_pto=sc. Accessed July 25, 2022.

59. "Atlético Confirms Cuca's Return to Command the Team," *News Bulletin 24/7.com* (July 23, 2022). https://newsbulletin247.com /sports/139386.html. Accessed July 26, 2022.

60. The phrase "dramatic happening" is from Michael DeLand's "A Sociology of the 'and One!': The Culture of Charisma in Pickup Basketball," *American Journal of Cultural Sociology* 10, no. 4 (December 2022): 677. Also see Eduardo Araripe Pacheco de Souza, "Fazer alianças: Uma escolha determinante entre o protagonismo e a invisibilidade dos grupos organizados de torcedores de futebol no Brasil" (Ph.D. dissertation in Anthropology, Universidade Federal de Pernambuco, 2016), 211.

61. Jefferson Nicassio Queiroga de Aquino, "O torcer no futebol como possibilidade de lazer e vínculo identitário para torcedores de América-MG, Atlético-MG e Cruzeiro" (Dissertação de Mestrado, Escola de Educação Física, Fisioterapia e Terapia Ocupacional, Universidade Federal de Minas Gerais, 2017), 34–35, 36–38, 70–71. As of 2017, CAM counted 75,305 avowed organized supporters, the seventh most at all levels of Brazilian *futebol*.

62. Hilário Franco Júnior, "Futebol, sociedade, cultura: Apontamentos a título de conclusão," in *Futebol objeto das ciências humanas*, ed. Flavio de Campos and Daniela Alfonsi (São Paulo: Leya, 2014), 368–369.

63. Interview with Alice Quintão Soares.

64. Franco Júnior, "Futebol, sociedade, cultura."

65. In Portuguese, the original words were *"Tudo o que é feito com amor obtém sucesso. Eu semore joguei futebol com amor"* (Everything that is done with love is successful. I have always played football with love). From "Tiro direto," *Jornal dos Sports* (August 6, 1985): 13.

66. Adriano Coelho, "Ciganos do futebol: Dadá Maravilha e Cláudio Adão," *Torcedores.com* (August 30, 2017). https://www.torcedores.com /noticias/2017/08/ciganos-dada-maravilha-e-claudio-adao. Accessed August 4, 2022.

67. This was even the case when Dario split his first two spells with CAM with a stint at Flamengo from 1973 to 1974, before the carioca side became a perennial thorn in the side of CAM. See "Dario quer voltar a ser a Dadá Maravilha," *Jornal dos Sports* (August 13, 1974): 12.

68. "Provêrbios do Dadá Maravilha," *Jornal dos Sports* (September 13, 1979): 2.

69. Ibid.

70. "Passe curto," *Jornal dos Sports* (June 29, 1984): 4.

71. Washington Rodrigues, "A volta de Nunes," *Jornal dos Sports* (July 17, 1984): 5.

72. "Máximas do futebol," *Jornal dos Sports* (September 16, 2002): 10.

73. "Máximas do futebol," *Jornal dos Sports* (October 25, 2002): 10.

74. "Máximas do futebol," *Jornal dos Sports* (October 21, 2003): 8.

75. "Dario quer voltar."
76. Interview with Paulo Roberto Prestes. Praça da Liberdade—Belo Horizonte, Brazil. August 9, 2022.
77. Ibid.
78. Ibid.
79. Ibid.
80. Ibid.
81. Interview with Heleno Oliveira. Assembleia Legislativa de Minas Gerais—Belo Horizonte, Brazil. August 10, 2022.
82. Ibid.
83. Ibid.
84. Interview with Rafael Miranda.
85. Ibid.

Chapter 4

1. The original Portuguese from João Guimarães Rosa's inaugural collection of short fiction reads, "*Era, outra vez em quando, a alegria*" (There was, once in a while, joy).
2. Betsy Reed, "'We Are for Democracy': Brazil Football Fans Clear Pro-Bolsonaro Blockades," *The Guardian* (November 2, 2022). https://www.the guardian.com/world/2022/nov/02/brazil-bolsonaro-football-protest-roads -cleared. Accessed July 26, 2023.
3. Franco Júnior, "Ensaio bibliográfico," 370.
4. Wisnik, *Veneno remédio*, 172.
5. Norbert Elias, *The Civilizing Process: Sociogenetic and Psychogenetic Investigations*, trans. Edmund Jephcott (New York: Urizen Books, 1978), 6.
6. Pedro Augusto Correia, "Manhã deste domingo tem manifestações pró e contra Bolsonaro em Belo Horizonte," *Otempo* (May 31, 2020). https://www.otempo.com.br/politica/manha-deste-domingo-tem-man ifestacoes-pro-e-contra-bolsonaro-em-belo-horizonte-1.2344077. Accessed July 26, 2023. Refer as well to Jorge Knijnik and Luiz Guilherme Burlamaqui, "From Football Nation to COVID 19-Land: Cultural Pedagogies and Political Protests during Syndemic Times in Brazil," in *Sport and Physical Culture in Global Pandemic Times*, ed. David L. Andrews, Holly Thorpe, and Joshua I. Newman (London: Palgrave Macmillan, 2023), 420, 423, 426–427. Knijnik and Burlamaqui remind us that it did not take the arrival of COVID-19 in 2020 to encourage coordination and cooperation among different *torcida* organizations in Brazil. As early as 2014, the fan groups of an assortment of club sides in Brazilian *futebol* formed the National Association of *Torcidas Organizadas* (Anatorg) to help soften the rivalries between teams while also creating a united front to influence sports policy and the politics of civil society at regional and national levels.

7. Eduardo Magalhães Souto Maior, "Impacto da pandemia na quantidade de gols na primeira divisão do Campeonato Brasileiro de Futebol." Trabalho de Conclusão de Curso (Bacharelado em Educação Física—Universidade Federal de Pernambuco, Recife, 2022), 18; Lucas de Albuquerque Freire, Márcio Tannure, Márcio Sampaio, Maamer Slimani, Hela Znazen, Nicola Luigi Bragazzi, Esteban Aedo-Muñoz, Dany Alexis Sobarzo Soto, Ciro José Brito, and Bianca Miarka, "COVID-19-Related Restrictions and Quarantine COVID-19: Effects on Cardiovascular and Yo-Yo Test Performance in Professional Soccer Players," *Frontiers in Psychology* 11 (December 2020): 1–8; and M. P. Pereira Lopes and J. L. Walczak, "Impacto da COVID-19 e o acúmulo de jogos das equipes do campeonato Brasileiro da Série A em 2021," *Revista Brasileira de Futsal e Futebol* 14 (2022): 147–153.

8. Richard Giulianotti, "Civilizing Games: Norbert Elias and the Sociology of Sport," in *Sport and Modern Social Theorists* (London: Palgrave Macmillan, 2004), 151.

9. Wisnik, *Veneno remédio*, 46.

10. Ibid., 120.

11. Wisnik's *futebol* love, it should be stated, is the São Paulo side Santos, not Clube Atlético Mineiro (CAM).

12. João Guimarães Rosa, "As margens da alegria," *Primeiras estórias* (Rio de Janeiro: Livraria José Olympio Editôra, 1962), 7. For more on Rosa's supposed affiliation with CAM, see Fred Melo Paiva, "Guimarães Rosa, 'o nosso Atlético' e o 9 a 2 eterno," *Da Arquibancada* (March 31, 2018). https://www-superesportes-com-br.translate.goog/app/1,669/2018/03/31 /se-coluna_fred_melo_interna,465567/guimaraes-rosa-o-nosso-atletico -e-o-9-a-2-eterno.shtml?_x_tr_sl=pt&_x_tr_tl=en&_x_tr_hl=en&_x_tr _pto=op,sc. Accessed July 4, 2022.

13. Interview with Ricardo Galuppo. São Paulo, Brazil (Zoom). July 19, 2022.

14. Galuppo, *Raça e amor*, 89.

15. "Die Brasilianer wurden klar geschlagen," *Arbeiter-Zeitung* (November 16, 1950): 8.

16. Jutta Braun, "So kalt! Als der brasilianische Fußball nach Deutschland kam—Die Eismeister," *11 Freunde* (July 10, 2014). https://11freunde .de/artikel/so-kalt-als-der-brasilianische-fussball-nach-deutschland-kam. Accessed July 27, 2022.

17. "De passagem o Atlético," *Jornal dos Sports* (December 14, 1950): 1; and "Confirmou na Europa o prestígio do futebol Brasileiro," *Diário de Minas* (December 19, 1950): 6.

18. "Confirmou na Europa o prestígio do futebol Brasileiro," 6.

19. "Vencedor o Atlético em Paris sob chuva e tremendo frio," *O Globo* (December 8, 1950): 12.

20. "Confirmou na Europa o prestígio do futebol brasileiro."
21. Filme n. 196—Teófilo Otoni—Cotidiano—*Família e futebol* (1957). Arquivo Público Mineiro, Belo Horizonte, Brazil.
22. Daniel L. McDonald, "The Origins of Informality in a Brazilian Planned City: Belo Horizonte, 1889–1900," *Journal of Urban History* 47, no. 1 (2021): 30–31; and Marshall C. Eakin, *Tropical Capitalism: The Industrialization of Belo Horizonte, Brazil, 1897–1997* (New York: Palgrave, 2001), 59–88.
23. "Constant Rise in Population," *Brazilian Bulletin* (August 15, 1957): 1–2.
24. Interview with Reinaldo.
25. The website "Remembering Reinaldo" is only one venue where Reinaldo's greatest "plays" can be watched. See https://playrface.co.uk /remembering-reinaldo/. Accessed May 4, 2022.
26. Grant Farred, *In Motion, at Rest: The Event of the Athletic Body* (Minneapolis: University of Minnesota Press, 2014), 2–3, 71–72.
27. Headquartered in Zurich, Switzerland, FIFA currently represents 211 affiliated football associations around the world, most of which represent internationally recognized nation-states.
28. In a bizarre sequence of events in March 2020, Ronaldinho and his brother were arrested in Paraguay after appearing in the country while holding false passports. Authorities held the brothers under house arrest in a luxury hotel in Paraguay's capital, Asunción, until August, when the accused were finally released. See "Ex-Barcelona and Brazil Star Ronaldinho Released from Paraguay Prison after Five Months," *ESPN.com* (August 24, 2020). https://www.espn.com/soccer/story/_/id/37585879/ex-barcelona-brazil-star-ronaldinho-released-paraguay-prison-five-months. Accessed August 6, 2023.
29. Interview with Rodolfo Gropen.
30. James Young, "Ronaldinho's Confounding Mexico Move Likely Motivated by Money," *SportsIllustrated.com* (September 6, 2014). https:// www.si.com/soccer/2014/09/06/ronaldinho-queretaro-fc-mexico-brazil -atletico-mineiro. Accessed May 13, 2022.
31. Fred Ribeiro, "Ronaldinho no Atlético-MG: Gropen revela pontos cruciais da reunião que selou o 'sim' entre R10 e Galo," *Globo.com* (June 4, 2022). Accessed July 8, 2022.
32. Interview with Rodolfo Gropen.
33. Ribeiro, "Ronaldinho no Atlético-MG."
34. "Ronaldinho Thanks Fans for Mother's Tribute," *sportskeeda* (September 24, 2012). https://www.sportskeeda.com/football/ronaldinho -thanks-fans-for-mothers-tribute. Accessed July 13, 2022.
35. Ibid.
36. Young, "Ronaldinho's Confounding Mexico Move."

37. Adriana Garcia, "Barcelona's Messi Sends Message to Ronaldinho after Mother's Death Due to COVID-19," *ESPN.com* (February 22, 2021). https://www.espn.com/soccer/barcelona/story/4321612/barcelonas-messi-sends-message-to-ronaldinho-after-mothers-death-due-to-covid-19. Accessed July 31, 2022.

38. Alessandro Zir, "Ontological Excess and Metonymy in Early Modern Descriptions of Brazil: Narratives of the Implausible," *Scripta Uniandrade* 15, no. 1 (2017): 187–188. For a fictional dramatization of Brazil's (and imperial Portugal's) early modern "excess," see João Ubaldo Ribeiro's novel *Viva o povo Brasileiro* (Rio de Janeiro: Editora Nova Fronteira, 1984).

39. Tariq Panja, "A Brazilian Soccer Giant Is Running a Player Farm in Eastern Europe," *Bloomberg* (February 15, 2017). https://www.bloomberg.com/news/features/2017-02-15/how-brazil-s-soccer-factory-dominates-a-5-billion-export-market. Accessed August 1, 2022.

40. Galeano, *Soccer in Sun and Shadow*, 2.

41. Fabricio Falkowski, "Inter vai ao ataque contra o São José," *Correio do Povo* (March 15, 2008): Inside cover.

42. The line reads in the original Portuguese "*Se houver uma camisa branca e preta pendurade no varal durante uma tempestade, o atleticano torce contra o vento.*"

43. Silva and Guimarães consider this story from a linguistic perspective in their essay "The Constitution of Brazilian Footballing Speech Objects," 87.

44. Tim Milnes, "Beyond Excess: Romanticism, Surplus, and Trust," *College Literature* 42, no. 4 (Fall 2015): 690.

45. Although he played for a spell at América Mineiro, Afonsinho never appeared for Atlético over the course of a career that saw him affiliated professionally with no fewer than seven different clubs. See Robert M. Levine, "Sport and Society: The Case of Brazilian Futebol," *Luso-Brazilian Review* 17, no. 2 (Winter 1980): 245–246.

46. Allison Margaret Bigelow and Thomas Miller Klubock, "Introduction to Latin American Studies and the Humanities: Past, Present, Future," *Latin American Research Review* 53, no. 3 (2018): 577.

47. Cássio Eduardo Viana Hissa, "A escrita com os pés," *Aletria* 22, no. 2 (2012): 55.

48. João Victor Marques, "Atlético joga mal e é goleado pelo Internacional na reestreia de Cuca," *superesportes.com* (July 31, 2022). https://www.mg.superesportes.com.br/app/noticias/futebol/atletico-mg/2022/07/31/noticia_atletico_mg,3973772/atletico-joga-mal-e-e-goleado-pelo-internacional-na-reestreia-de-cuca.shtml. Accessed August 2, 2022.

49. Normally, the Campeonato Brasileiro Série A would run until December. With the 2022 FIFA World Cup having been rescheduled from

summer to late fall, however, to adjust for the high temperatures of host nation Qatar, the Brasileirão, like football leagues around the globe, altered its domestic schedule to accommodate the much-anticipated international tournament.

50. WhatsApp chat with Luiz Silva, August 1, 2022.

51. Ibid.

52. CAM Instagram account, https://www.instagram.com/atletico/. Accessed August 11, 2022.

Appendix

1. Clifford Geertz, "Deep Play: Notes on the Balinese Cockfight," *Daedalus* 101, no. 1 (Winter 1972): 15.

2. Hamayon, *Why We Play*, 14. Offering original insights of his own, Roger Caillois continues Johan Huizinga's work on play in his book *Les jeux et les hommes* (1958).

3. Robert Anchor, "History and Play: Johan Huizinga and His Critics," *History and Theory* 17, no. 1 (February 1978): 64–65.

4. Ibid., 85–86. Original emphasis.

5. Ibid., 79.

6. Geertz calls play a form of "metasocial commentary" and likens the cockfighting he observed to a "Balinese reading of Balinese experience; a story they [the Balinese] tell themselves about themselves" ("Deep Play," 26). Stephen Nachmanovitch similarly describes play as a form of "meta-communication: a communication that tells the receiver how to interpret what is received." From Nachmanovitch's "This Is Play," *New Literary History* 40, no. 1 (Winter 2009): 1–2.

7. Hamayon, *Why We Play*, 8.

8. Ibid., xvii.

9. Ibid., 4. For more on Norbert Elias's contributions to the scholarly discussion of play, see Giulianotti, "Civilizing Games," 145, 151.

10. Trygve B. Broch, "The Cultural Sociology of Sport: A Study of Sports for Sociology?," *American Journal of Cultural Sociology* 10, no. 4 (December 2022): 536.

11. Ibid., 536–537.

12. Elias acknowledges the contradictory forces that are involved in *sports* play when he writes of the "pleasurable" capacity sport has for the "de-controlling of human feelings" and "the maintenance" that is thereby required in society for "a set of checks to keep the pleasantly de-controlled emotions under control." See Elias, "Introduction," in Norbert Elias and Eric Dunning, *Quest for Excitement: Sport and Leisure in the Civilising Process* (Oxford: Blackwell, 1986), 49.

13. Hamayon, *Why We Play*, 67–68.

14. Eduardo P. Archetti, "The Meaning of Sport in Anthropology: A View from Latin America," *European Review of Latin American and Caribbean Studies* 65 (December 1998): 99, 101.

15. Douglas Hartmann, *Midnight Basketball: Race, Sports, and Neoliberal Social Policy* (Chicago: University of Chicago Press, 2016), 86. For a comparable basketball-themed project, see DeLand's "A Sociology of the 'and One!,'" 676–703. Of particular interest are what DeLand describes as the "emotional logic" of his "empirical ethnographic materials," which comprise the author's observations of a local pickup basketball game in Santa Monica, California (677–678).

16. Corte, *Dangerous Fun*, 81, 83.

17. For a full accounting of the pandemic's impact on world sports (and the scholarship that continues to be written on the same), see the essay collection *Sport and Physical Culture in Global Pandemic Times*, edited by David L. Andrews, Holly Thorpe, and Joshua I. Newman (London: Palgrave Macmillan, 2023).

18. DeLand, "A Sociology of the 'and One!,'" 676.

19. Corte, *Dangerous Fun*, 81.

20. Ibid., 83; and Randall Collins, "Stratification, Emotional Energy, and the Transient Emotions," in *Research Agendas in the Sociology of Emotions*, ed. Theodore D. Kemper (Albany: State University of New York Press, 1990), 28.

Bibliography

Primary Sources

Interviews

Frederico Bolivar. Lisbon, Portugal (Zoom). June 3, 2022.
Ricardo Galuppo. São Paulo, Brazil (Zoom). July 19, 2022.
Rodolfo Gropen. Savassi—Belo Horizonte, Brazil. July 12, 2022.
Carol Leandro. Belo Horizonte, Brazil (Zoom). July 20, 2022.
João Leite. Assembleia Legislativa de Minas Gerais—Belo Horizonte, Brazil. August 10, 2022.
Márcio de Lima Leite. Casa Fiat de Cultura—Belo Horizonte, Brazil. July 21, 2022.
Helvécio Marins Jr. Lisbon, Portugal (Zoom). June 28, 2022.
Rafael Miranda. Belo Horizonte, Brazil (Zoom). August 12, 2022.
Nelinho. Sion—Belo Horizonte, Brazil. May 30, 2022.
Heleno Oliveira. Assembleia Legislativa de Minas Gerais—Belo Horizonte, Brazil. August 10, 2022.
Fred Melo Paiva. Caraíva, Brazil (Zoom). July 8, 2022.
Paulo Roberto Prestes. Praça da Liberdade—Belo Horizonte, Brazil. August 9, 2022.
Reinaldo. Palácio das Mangabeiras—Belo Horizonte, Brazil. June 3, 2022.
Réver. Belo Horizonte, Brazil (WhatsApp chat). June 27, 2022.
Alice Quintão Soares. Salvador, Brazil (Zoom). June 27, 2022.
Victor. Belo Horizonte, Brazil (WhatsApp chat). August 24, 2022.

Arquivo Público Mineiro
Filme n.196—Teófilo Otoni—Cotidiano—*Família e futebol* (1957).
Coleção Municípios Mineiros.

Print and Multimedia
Assis, Machado de. *Memorías póstumas de Brás Cubas* (1880; rept. São Paulo: Ateliê Editorial, 2004).
Avelar, Idelber. Galo supporter's website. http://www.tulane.edu/~avelar /galo.html. Accessed January 5, 2021.
"Die Brasilianer wurden klar geschlagen," *Arbeiter-Zeitung* (November 16, 1950): 8.
Braun, Jutta. "So kalt! Als der brasilianische Fußball nach Deutschland kam—Die Eismeister," *11 Freunde* (July 10, 2014). https://11freunde .de/artikel/so-kalt-als-der-brasilianische-fussball-nach-deutschland -kam. Accessed July 27, 2022.
Castro, Carlos Etiene de. "Moura Costa," *Jornal Estado de Minas* (April 2, 1950): 4.
"Confirmou na Europa o prestígio do futebol Brasileiro," *Diário de Minas* (December 19, 1950): 6.
O dia do Galo (2014), dir. Cris Azzi and Luiz Felipe Fernandes.
Filho, Mário. *O Negro no Futebol Brasileiro* (1947; rept. Rio de Janeiro: Mauad X, 2010).
Freyre, Gilberto. "Foot-ball mulatto," *Diário de Pernambuco* (June 17, 1938): 4.
Galo Na Veia. https://galonaveia.atletico.com.br/home. Accessed May 31, 2022.
Jornal dos Sports (Rio de Janeiro sports daily, 1931–2003).
Lutar, lutar, lutar (2021), dir. Sérgio Borges and Helvécio Marins Jr.
Márquez, Gabriel García. "El juramento" (1983), in *Copa América* (Buenos Aires: Plan Nacional de Lectura, 2011).
———. *Love in the Time of Cholera*, trans. Edith Grossman (1985; rept. New York: Penguin, 1989).
Neto, João Leite da Silva. *João Leite: O goleiro de deus em preto e branco* (Belo Horizonte: 2019).
"Remembering Reinaldo." https://playrface.co.uk/remembering-reinaldo/. Accessed May 4, 2022.
Ribeiro, João Ubaldo. *Viva o povo Brasileiro* (Rio de Janeiro: Editora Nova Fronteira, 1984).
Rodrigues, Nelson. *À sombra das chuteiras imortais: Crônicas de futebol*, ed. Ruy Castro (São Paulo: Companhia das Letra, 1993).
———. "História de Amor," *O Globo* (June 10, 1973): 2.
Rosa, João Guimarães. "As margens da alegria," *Primeiras estórias* (Rio de Janeiro: Livraria José Olympio Editôra, 1962): 1–7.
Schiller, Friedrich. *Letters on the Aesthetic Education of Man*, trans.

Reginald Snell (1794; rept. Mineola, NY: Dover Publications, 2004).

Stein, Gertrude. *Geography and Plays*, ed. Cyrena N. Pondrom (Madison: University of Wisconsin Press, 1993).

"Vencedor o atlético em Paris sob chuva e tremendo frio," *O Globo* (December 8, 1950): 12.

Whitman, Walt. *Leaves of Grass* (Brooklyn, New York, 1855).

Yes We C.A.M. (2013). https://www.youtube.com/watch?v=lryHgGAO -o8. Accessed May 8, 2022.

Secondary Sources

Alves, Fábio Padilha. "Amor à camisa? Conciliando razão e paixão no ambiente do futebol professional" (Dissertações de mestrado, Programa de Pós-Graduação em Educação Física, Universidade Federal do Espírito Santo, 2010).

Alves, Marcus. "Evangelicalism and Brazil: The Religious Movement That Spread through a National Team," *BBC Sport* (March 22, 2022). https:// www.bbc.com/sport/football/60483820. Accessed August 13, 2022.

Anchor, Robert. "History and Play: Johan Huizinga and His Critics," *History and Theory* 17, no. 1 (February 1978): 63–93.

Aquino, Jefferson Nicassio Queiroga de. "O torcer no futebol como possibilidade de lazer e vínculo identitário para torcedores de América-MG, Atlético-MG e Cruzeiro" (Dissertação de Mestrado, Escola de Educação Física, Fisioterapia e Terapia Ocupacional, Universidade Federal de Minas Gerais, 2017).

Archetti, Eduardo P. "The Meaning of Sport in Anthropology: A View from Latin America," *European Review of Latin American and Caribbean Studies* 65 (December 1998): 91–103.

Arruda, Gabriela Alcantara Azevedo Cavalcanti de, Daniel Medeiros de Freitas, Carolina Maria Soares Lima, Krzysztof Nawratek, and Bernardo Miranda Pataro. "The Production of Knowledge through Religious and Social Media Infrastructure: World Making Practices among Brazilian Pentecostals," *Popular Communication* (May 4, 2022): 1–14.

Atkinson, Michael. "Interview(s) with the Vampire: Research Opportunism during a Global Catastrophe," in *Sport and Physical Culture in Global Pandemic Times*, ed. David L. Andrews, Holly Thorpe, and Joshua I. Newman (London: Palgrave Macmillan, 2023), 771–795.

"Atlético Confirms Cuca's Return to Command the Team," *News Bulletin 24/7.com* (July 23, 2022). https://newsbulletin247.com/sports/139386 .html. Accessed July 26, 2022.

"Atlético-MG mantém escrita sobre o Flamengo em Minas," *The Lance!* (June 19, 2022). https://www.lance.com.br/atletico-mineiro/atletico -mg-mantem-escrita-sobre-o-flamengo-em-minas-e-turco-mohamed -ganha-folego-com-vitoria.html. Accessed June 20, 2022.

Bellos, Alex. *Futebol: The Brazilian Way of Life* (New York: Bloomsbury, 2002).

Bercovitch, Sacvan. "The Problem of Ideology in American Literary History," *Critical Inquiry* 12, no. 4 (Summer 1986): 631–653.

Bergen, Doris. "Psychological Approaches to the Study of Play," *American Journal of Play* 7, no. 3 (Fall 2015): 101–128.

Bernstein, Charles. "Gertrude Stein," in *A History of Modernist Poetry*, ed. Alex Davis and Lee M. Jenkins (New York: Cambridge University Press, 2015), 255–274.

Bigelow, Allison Margaret, and Thomas Miller Klubock. "Introduction to Latin American Studies and the Humanities: Past, Present, Future," *Latin American Research Review* 53, no. 3 (2018): 573–580.

Birrell, Susan. "Sport as Ritual: Interpretations from Durkheim to Goffman," *Social Forces* 60, no. 2 (December 1981): 354–376.

"The Bolsa Família Program," in *The Brazil Reader: History, Culture, Politics*, ed. James N. Green, Victoria Langland, and Lilia Moritz Schwarcz (Durham: Duke University Press, 2019), 523–525.

Braidotti, Rosi. "We Are in This Together, but We Are Not One and the Same," *Journal of Bioethical Inquiry* 17, no. 4 (2020): 465–469.

"Brazil Scrambles to Approve Coronavirus Vaccine as Pressure Mounts," *Los Angeles Times* (January 1, 2021). https://www.latimes.com/world -nation/story/2021-01-01/brazil-scrambles-to-approve-virus-vaccine -as-pressure-mounts. Accessed January 6, 2021.

Broch, Trygve B. "The Cultural Sociology of Sport: A Study of Sports for Sociology?," *American Journal of Cultural Sociology* 10, no. 4 (December 2022): 535–542.

Bucher, Bernd, and Julian Eck. "Football's Contribution to International Order: The Ludic and Festive Reproduction of International Society by World Societal Actors," *International Theory* (2021): 1–27.

Burke, Kenneth. "Literature as Equipment for Living," in *The Philosophy of Literary Form: Studies in Symbolic Action* (Baton Rouge: Louisiana State University Press, 1941), 292–304.

Burnett, Stephanie. "Mick Jagger Is Being Blamed for Brazil's World Cup Thrashing," *Time* (July 9, 2014). https://time.com/2968373/world -cup-brazil-mick-jagger-football-soccer/. Accessed June 19, 2022.

"Campeonato Brasileiro de 1937: Saiba como foi o Torneio dos Campeões que o Atlético-MG venceu," *The Lance!* (August 25, 2023). https:// www.lance.com.br/atletico-mineiro/campeonato-brasileiro-de-1937 -saiba-como-foi-o-torneio-dos-campeoes-que-o-atletico-mg-venceu .html. Accessed August 26, 2023.

Campo, Mickael, Diane M. Mackie, and Xavier Sanchez. "Emotions in Group Sports: A Narrative Review from a Social Identity Perspective," *Frontiers in Psychology* 10 (2019): 666–682.

Carrington, Ben. *Race, Sport and Politics: The Sporting Black Diaspora* (London: SAGE, 2010).

Carvalho, Bruno. "O que se sabe sobre o caso envolvendo Cuca na Suíça," *UOL* (March 3, 2021). https://www.uol.com.br/esporte/futebol /ultimas-noticias/2021/03/03/o-que-se-sabe-sobre-o-caso-envolvendo -cuca-na-suica-em-1987.htm. Accessed June 24, 2023.

Carvalho, Martha de Ulhôa. "Canção da América—Style and Emotion in Brazilian Popular Song," *Popular Music 9*, no. 3 (October 1990): 321–349.

"City Football Group Bid for Atlético Mineiro," *Reuters* (March 22, 2022). https://www.reuters.com/markets/funds/city-football-group-bid-atle tico-mineiro-report-2022-03-07/. Accessed May 14, 2022.

Coelho, Adriano. "Ciganos do futebol: Dadá Maravilha e Cláudio Adão," *Torcedores.com* (August 30, 2017). https://www.torcedores.com /noticias/2017/08/ciganos-dada-maravilha-e-claudio-adao. Accessed August 4, 2022.

Collins, Randall. "Stratification, Emotional Energy, and the Transient Emotions," in *Research Agendas in the Sociology of Emotions*, ed. Theodore D. Kemper (Albany: State University of New York Press, 1990), 27–57.

"Constant Rise in Population," *Brazilian Bulletin* (August 15, 1957): 1–2.

Cornacchione, Edgard, and Liliane Klaus. "Ethical Business Culture in Brazil: Advantages and Obstacles of National *Jeitinho*," in *Ethical Business Cultures in Emerging Markets*, ed. Douglas Jondle and Alexandre Ardichvili (New York: Cambridge University Press, 2017), 9–27.

Cornelsen, Elcio Loureiro. "Futebol em tempos de pandemia, ontem e hoje," *Ludopédio* 129 (March 2020): 1–10.

———. "Futebol e narrativa—Desafios para a literatura," *Ludopédio* 114 (December 15, 2018): 10.

———. "Imagens do negro no futebol Brasileiro," *Vozes, Pretérito e Devir 5*, no. 1 (2016): 77–98.

———. "Memória e futebol no Brasil—Escritas da vida de jogadores Bras-ileiros," *História: Questões and Debates* 68, no. 2 (2020): 133–159.

———. "Protagonistas e coadjuvantes—Um olhar para o desempenho de clubes no Campeonato Brasileiro da Série A (2010–2019)," *Ludopédio* 114 (May 17, 2021): 1–12.

Cornelsen, Elcio, and Erilma Desiree da Silva. "A trilha sonora dos times das gerais," *Suplemento: O Futebol no Campo das Letras* (June 2014): 28–29.

Correia, Pedro Augusto. "Manhã deste domingo tem manifestações pró e contra Bolsonaro em Belo Horizonte," *Otempo* (May 31, 2020). https://www.otempo.com.br/politica/manha-deste-domingo-tem

-manifestacoes-pro-e-contra-bolsonaro-em-belo-horizonte-1.2344077. Accessed July 26, 2023.

Corte, Ugo. *Dangerous Fun: The Social Lives of Big Wave Surfers* (Chicago: University of Chicago Press, 2022).

Crosara Junior, Ademar. "A identificação com o time, a curiosidade específica do torcedor e a satisfação do torcedor como antecedentes da intenção de compra do torcedor de futebol no Brasil" (Dissertação, Programa de Pós-graduação em Administração, Universidade Federal de Uberlândia, 2016).

DaMatta, Roberto. "Sport in Society: An Essay on Brazilian Football," *VIBRANT* 6, no. 2 (December 2009): 98–120.

DeLand, Michael. "A Sociology of the 'and One!': The Culture of Charisma in Pickup Basketball," *American Journal of Cultural Sociology* 10, no. 4 (December 2022): 676–703.

Dimock, Wai Chee. "Gaming the Pandemic," *PMLA* 136, no. 2 (March 2021): 163–170.

Ducca, Caio, Cássio Arreguy, Clara Arreguy, Daniel Van R. de Lima, and Philipe Van R. de Lima. *Nós somos do Clube Atlético Mineiro: A história do Galo* (São Paulo: Onze Cultural, 2022).

Eakin, Marshall C. *Tropical Capitalism: The Industrialization of Belo Horizonte, Brazil, 1897–1997* (New York: Palgrave, 2001).

Eco, Umberto. "Sports Chatter" (1969), in *Travels in Hyperreality: Essays*, trans. William Weaver (New York: Harcourt Brace Jovanovich, 1986), 159–166.

Elias, Norbert. *The Civilizing Process: Sociogenetic and Psychogenetic Investigations*, trans. Edmund Jephcott (New York: Urizen Books, 1978).

Elias, Norbert, and Eric Dunning. *Quest for Excitement: Sport and Leisure in the Civilising Process* (Oxford: Blackwell, 1986).

"Eliminado, Atlético-MG deixa escapar prêmio milionário e fecha a Copa do Brasil com R$4,9 milhões," *Globo.com* (July 14, 2022). https://ge.globo.com/futebol/times/atletico-mg/noticia/2022/07/14/eliminado-atletico-mg-deixa-escapar-premio-milionario-e-fecha-a-copa-do-brasil-com-r-49-milhoes.ghtml. Accessed July 16, 2022.

Elsey, Brenda, and Joshua Nadel. *Futbolera: A History of Women and Sports in Latin America* (Austin: University of Texas Press, 2019).

"Ex-Barcelona and Brazil star Ronaldinho released from Paraguay prison after five months," *ESPN.com* (August 24, 2020). https://www.espn.com/soccer/story/_/id/37585879/ex-barcelona-brazil-star-ronaldinho-released-paraguay-prison-five-months. Accessed August 6, 2023.

Falkowski, Fabricio. "Inter vai ao ataque contra o São José," *Correio do Povo* [Porto Alegre] (March 15, 2008): Inside cover.

Fanon, Frantz. *Black Skin, White Masks*, trans. Charles Lam Markmann (1952; rept. New York: Grove Press, 1967).

Farred, Grant. *In Motion, at Rest: The Event of the Athletic Body* (Minneapolis: University of Minnesota Press, 2014).

———. *Long Distance Love: A Passion for Football* (Philadelphia: Temple University Press, 2008).

———. *Only a Black Athlete Can Save Us Now* (Minneapolis: University of Minnesota Press, 2022).

Flusser, Vilém. *Fenomenologia do Brasileiro: Em busca de um novo homem*, org. and trans. Gustavo Bernardo (Rio de Janeiro: Editora da Universidade do Estado do Rio de Janeiro, 1998).

Foer, Franklin. *How Soccer Explains the World: An Unlikely Theory of Globalization* (New York: HarperCollins, 2004).

Franco Júnior, Hilário. *A dança dos deuses: Futebol, cultura, sociedade* (São Paulo: Companhia das Letras, 2007).

Frazier, Ian. "Rereading 'Lolita,'" *The New Yorker* (December 14, 2020): 30–35.

Freire, Lucas de Albuquerque, Márcio Tannure, Márcio Sampaio, Maamer Slimani, Hela Znazen, Nicola Luigi Bragazzi, Esteban Aedo-Muñoz, Dany Alexis Sobarzo Soto, Ciro José Brito, and Bianca Miarka. "COVID-19-Related Restrictions and Quarantine COVID-19: Effects on Cardiovascular and Yo-Yo Test Performance in Professional Soccer Players," *Frontiers in Psychology* 11 (December 2020): 1–8.

Galeano, Eduardo. *Soccer in Sun and Shadow* (1995; rept. New York: Verso, 1999).

Galuppo, Ricardo. *Raça e amor: A saga do Clube Atlético Mineiro vista da arquibancada* (São Paulo: DBA Editora, 2005).

Garcia, Adriana. "Barcelona's Messi Sends Message to Ronaldinho after Mother's Death Due to COVID-19," *ESPN.com* (February 22, 2021). https://www.espn.com/soccer/barcelona/story/4321612/barcelonas-messi-sends-message-to-ronaldinho-after-mothers-death-due-to-covid-19. Accessed July 31, 2022.

———. "Milan Court: Robinho 'Brutally Humiliated' Victim," *ESPN. com* (March 10, 2021). https://www.espn.com/soccer/acmilan/story/4334518/milan-court-robinho-brutally-humiliated-rape-victim. Accessed July 24, 2023.

Garcia, Diego, Marcus Alves, and Rafael Valente. "Dos grandes, só Palmeiras não aderiu ao parcelamento de dívida com a união," *ESPN.com.br* (November 25, 2015). http://www.espn.com.br/noticia/560080_dos-grandes-so-palmeiras-nao-aderiu-ao-parcelamento-de-divida-com-a-uniao. Accessed May 15, 2022.

Geertz, Clifford. "Deep Play: Notes on the Balinese Cockfight," *Daedalus* 101, no. 1 (Winter 1972): 1–37.

Giulianotti, Richard. "Civilizing Games: Norbert Elias and the Sociology of Sport," in *Sport and Modern Social Theorists* (London: Palgrave Macmillan, 2004), 145–160.

Goldblatt, David. *The Age of Football: Soccer and the 21st Century* (New York: Norton, 2020).

———. *Futebol Nation: A Footballing History of Brazil* (London: Penguin, 2014).

Gumbrecht, Hans Ulrich. *In Praise of Athletic Beauty* (Cambridge, MA: Belknap Press of Harvard University Press, 2006).

Günther, Augustin. "Kant no Brasil—Fora do lugar?" *Impulso* 19, no. 47 (2009): 75–85.

Hall, Stuart. "Race, the Floating Signifier: What More Is There to Say about 'Race'?," in *Selected Writings on Race and Difference*, ed. Paul Gilroy and Ruth Wilson Gilmore (Durham: Duke University Press, 2021), 359–373.

Hamayon, Roberte. *Why We Play: An Anthropological Study*, trans. Damien Simon (2012; rept. Chicago: HAU Books, 2016).

Harris, Kara, Angel D. Armenta, Christine Reyna, and Michael A. Zárate. "Latinx Stereotypes: Myths and Realities in the Twenty-First Century," in *Stereotypes: The Incidence and Impacts of Bias*, ed. Elora C. Voyles and Joel T. Nadler (Westport, CT: Greenwood Publishing Group, 2020), 128–145.

Hartmann, Douglas. *Midnight Basketball: Race, Sports, and Neoliberal Social Policy* (Chicago: University of Chicago Press, 2016).

Hein, Hilde. "Play as an Aesthetic Concept," *Journal of Aesthetics and Art Criticism* 27, no. 1 (Autumn 1968): 67–71.

Helal, Ronaldo, and Cesar Gordon Jr. "Sociologia, história e romance na construção da indentidade nacional através do futebol," in Ronaldo Helal, Antônio Jorge Soares, and Hugo Lovisolo, *A invenção do país do futebol: Mídia, raça e idolatria* (Rio de Janeiro: Mauad, 2012), 51–73.

Hissa, Cássio Eduardo Viana. "A escrita com os pés," *Aletria* 22, no. 2 (2012): 45–57.

Hollanda, Bernardo Buarque de. "The Competitive Party: The Formation and Crisis of Organized Fan Groups in Brazil, 1950–1980," in *Football and the Boundaries of History: Critical Studies in Soccer*, ed. Brenda Elsey and Stanislao G. Pugliese (New York: Palgrave Macmillan, 2017), 295–312.

Holowchak, Mark. "Freud on Play, Games, and Sports Fanaticism," *Journal of the American Academy of Psychoanalysis and Dynamic Psychiatry* 39, no. 4 (2011): 695–715.

Horch, Dan. "Brazilian Soccer's Financial Disarray Starts to Show on the Field," *New York Times* (April 23, 2015). https://www.nytimes .com/2015/04/24/sports/soccer/brazilian-soccers-financial-disarray -starts-to-show-on-the-field.html. Accessed May 15, 2022.

Huizinga, Johan. *Homo Ludens: A Study of the Play-Element in Culture* (1938; rept. London: Routledge, 2003).

Jackson, Gregory E. "*Malandros*: 'Honourable Workers' and the

Professionalization of Brazilian Football, 1930–1950," in *The Country of Football: Politics, Popular Culture, and the Beautiful Game in Brazil*, ed. Paulo Fontes and Bernardo Borges Buarque de Hollanda (London: Hurst, 2014), 41–66.

James, C. L. R. *Beyond a Boundary* (1963; rept. Durham: Duke University Press, 2013).

Jones, Mark. "Bill Shankly's Famous 'Life and Death' Misquote and What Liverpool Icon Really Meant," *Mirror* (March 31, 2020). https://www.mirror.co.uk/sport/football/news/bill-shanklys-famous-life-death-21784583. Accessed July 16, 2022.

Jorge, Matheus Marinho, and Elcio Loureiro Cornelsen. "Dirceu Lopes, um expoente do futebol arte," *Ludopédio* 26 (September 24, 2019): 1–4.

Júnior, Hilário Franco. "Ensaio bibliográfico," *Revista de História* 163 (July–December 2010): 369–389.

———. "Futebol, sociedade, cultura: Apontamentos a título de conclusão," in *Futebol objeto das ciências humanas*, ed. Flavio de Campos and Daniela Alfonsi (São Paulo: Leya, 2014), 365–383.

Kittleson, Roger. *The Country of Football: Soccer and the Making of Modern Brazil* (Berkeley: University of California Press, 2014).

———. "Fausto dos Santos: The Wonders and Challenges of Blackness in Brazil's 'Mulatto Football,'" in *Football and the Boundaries of History: Critical Studies in Soccer*, ed. Brenda Elsey and Stanislao G. Pugliese (New York: Palgrave Macmillan, 2017), 161–178.

Knijnik, Jorge, and Luiz Guilherme Burlamaqui. "From Football Nation to COVID 19-Land: Cultural Pedagogies and Political Protests during Syndemic Times in Brazil," in *Sport and Physical Culture in Global Pandemic Times*, ed. David L. Andrews, Holly Thorpe, and Joshua I. Newman (London: Palgrave Macmillan, 2023), 419–443.

Kuper, Simon, and Stefan Szymanski. *Soccernomics: Why England Loses, Why Germany and Brazil Win, and Why the U.S., Japan, Australia, Turkey—And Even Iraq—Are Destined to Become the Kings of the World's Most Popular Sport* (New York: Nation Books, 2009).

Lacombe, Milly. "The whitening of Brazilian football according to the philosopher Sueli Carneiro," *UOL* (May 28, 2022). https://www.ruetir.com/2022/05/29/opinion-milly-lacombe-the-whitening-of-brazilian-football-according-to-philosopher-sueli-carneiro/. Accessed June 9, 2022.

"Leandro Castro Mora," *Galo Digital*. https://www-galodigital-com-br.translate.goog/enciclopedia/Leandro_Castilho_Moura_Costa?_x_tr_sch=http&_x_tr_sl=pt&_x_tr_tl=en&_x_tr_hl=en&_x_tr_pto=sc. Accessed June 30, 2022.

Lears, T. J. Jackson. *Something for Nothing: Luck in America* (New York: Viking, 2003).

Levine, Robert M. "Sport and Society: The Case of Brazilian Futebol," *Luso-Brazilian Review* 17, no. 2 (Winter 1980): 233–252.

Lima, Philipe Van R. *Punho cerrado: A história do Rei* (Belo Horizonte: Letramento, 2017).

Lopes, Felipe Tavares Paes, and Mariana Prioli Cordeiro. "Futebol, massa e poder: Reflexões sobre a 'teoria do contágio,'" *Psicologia Política* 15, no. 34 (2015): 479–495.

Lopes, M. P. Pereira, and J. L. Walczak. "Impacto da COVID-19 e o acúmulo de jogos das equipes do campeonato Brasileiro da Série A em 2021," *Revista Brasileira de Futsal e Futebol* 14 (2022): 147–153.

Lott, Eric. *Love and Theft: Blackface Minstrelsy and the American Working Class* (New York: Oxford University Press, 1993).

Maranhão, Tiago Fernandes, and Jorge Knijnik. "Futebol Mulato: Racial Constructs in Brazilian Football," *Cosmopolitan Civil Societies Journal* 3, no. 2 (2011): 55–71.

Marques, João Victor. "Atlético joga mal e é goleado pelo Internacional na reestreia de Cuca," *superesportes.com* (July 31, 2022). https://www.mg.superesportes.com.br/app/noticias/futebol/atletico-mg/2022/07/31/noticia_atletico_mg,3973772/atletico-joga-mal-e-e-goleado-pelo-internacional-na-reestreia-de-cuca.shtml. Accessed August 2, 2022.

Martins, André. "A positividade das alegrias partilhadas: Reflexões filosóficas sobre o arrebatamento pelo futebol como afirmação da vida, de nossa própria potência e da potência do coletivo," in *Uma bola no pé uma ideia na cabeça: O que o futebol nos faz pensar*, ed. Arthur L. F. Ferreira, André Martins, and Robert Segal (Rio de Janeiro: Editora Universidade Federal do Rio de Janeiro, 2014), 42, 81.

Martins, Cristiano. "Risco de morte por COVID é 46% maior entre a população negra em Minas Gerais," *Otempo* (July 10, 2020). https://www.otemp.com.br/cidades/risco-de-morte-por-covid-e-46-maior-entre-a-populacao-negra-em-minas-gerais-1.2358721. Accessed June 8, 2022.

McDonald, Daniel L. "The Origins of Informality in a Brazilian Planned City: Belo Horizonte, 1889–1900," *Journal of Urban History* 47, no. 1 (2021): 29–49.

Melo, Victor. "Olhares irônicos: Machado de Assis e o esporte," *Aletria* 26, no. 3 (2016): 123–140.

Mezzaroba, Cristiano. "O impulso lúdico, a experiência estética e a cultura midiática esportiva," *Revista Brasileira de Estudos do Lazer* 3, no. 1 (2016): 53–75.

O milagre do horto, ed. André Fidusi, Fernando Gregori, and Frederico Jota (São Paulo: Coletivo Editorial, 2016).

Milnes, Tim. "Beyond Excess: Romanticism, Surplus, and Trust," *College Literature* 42, no. 4 (Fall 2015): 683–698.

Mostaro, Filipe Fernandes Ribeiro, Ronaldo George Helal, and Fausto Amaro. "Futebol, nação e representações: A importância do estilo 'futebol-arte' na construção da identidade nacional," *História Unisinos* 19, no. 3 (2015): 272–282.

Nachmanovitch, Stephen. "This Is Play," *New Literary History* 40, no. 1 (Winter 2009): 1–24.

Ngai, Sianne. *Ugly Feelings* (Cambridge, MA: Harvard University Press, 2005).

Nunes, Felipe Alexandre de Souza Félix, and Jonathan Simões Freitas. "Combination of Factors for the Presence of the Public: A Look at the Lower Levels of Football in Minas Gerais," *Revista Intercontinental de Gestão* 11 (2021): 1–11.

Paiva, Fred Melo. "Uma chance para o acerto de contas do Galo com o Flamengo," *Jornal Estado de Minas* (July 9, 2022). https://www.em.com.br/app/colunistas/fred-melo-paiva/2022/07/09/interna_fred_melo_paiva,1378991/uma-chance-para-o-acerto-de-contas-do-galo-com-o-flamengo.shtml. Accessed July 9, 2022.

———. "Contra o Flamengo, grileiro dos nossos sonhos, a guerra," *Jornal Estado de Minas* (June 18, 2022). https://www.em.com.br/app/colunistas/fred-melo-paiva/2022/06/18/interna_fred_melo_paiva,1374116/contra-o-flamengo-grileiro-dos-nossos-sonhos-a-guerra.shtml. Accessed June 19, 2022.

———. "Guimarães Rosa, 'o nosso atlético' e o 9 a 2 eterno," *Da Arquibancada* (March 31, 2018). https://www-superesportes-com-br.translate.goog/app/1,669/2018/03/31/se-coluna_fred_melo_inte rna,465567/guimaraes-rosa-o-nosso-atletico-e-o-9-a-2-eterno.shtml?_x_tr_sl=pt&_x_tr_tl=en&_x_tr_hl=en&_x_tr_pto=op,sc. Accessed July 4, 2022.

Panja, Tariq. "A Brazilian Soccer Giant Is Running a Player Farm in Eastern Europe," *Bloomberg* (February 15, 2017). https://www.bloomberg.com/news/features/2017-02-15/how-brazil-s-soccer-factory-dom inates-a-5-billion-export-market. Accessed August 1, 2022.

Phillips, Dom. "Atlético Take Libertadores—Finally," *Folha de São Paulo* (July 25, 2013). https://www1.folha.uol.com.br/mundo/2013/07/1316852-from-brazil-atletico-take-libertadores—-finally.shtml. Accessed June 22, 2022.

Phillips, Tom. "'Lack of Shame': Robinho Scandal Highlights Brazil's Rape Crisis," *The Guardian* (October 22, 2020). https://www.theguardian.com/world/2020/oct/22/brazil-rape-robinho-santos. Accessed July 18, 2023.

Reed, Betsy. "'We Are for Democracy': Brazil Football Fans Clear Pro-Bolsonaro Blockades," *The Guardian* (November 2, 2022). https://www.theguardian.com/world/2022/nov/02/brazil-bolsonaro-football-protest-roads-cleared. Accessed July 26, 2023.

Ribeiro, Fred. "De torcedor a 'homem forte' do atlético: O choro dos filhos que mudou a vida de Rodolfo Gropen," *Hoje em Dia* (November 11, 2021). https://www.hojeemdia.com.br/esportes/de-torcedor-a -homem-forte-do-atletico-o-choro-dos-filhos-que-mudou-a-vida-de -rodolfo-gropen-1.425161. Accessed July 8, 2022.

———. "Ronaldinho no Atlético-MG: Gropen revela pontos cruciais da reunião que selou o 'sim' entre R10 e Galo," *Globo.com* (June 4, 2022) . https://ge.globo.com/futebol/times/atletico-mg/noticia/2022/06/04 /ronaldinho-no-atletico-mg-ex-diretor-revela-pontos-cruciais-da-re uniao-que-selou-o-sim-entre-r10-e-galo.ghtml. Accessed July 8, 2022.

———. "Without Forecasting to Vote on 2020 Balance Sheet, Atlético-MG Prepares Event to Show Financial Reality; Debt Exceeds R$1 Billion," *Globo.com* (March 26, 2021). https://globoesporte.globo.com/futebol /times/atletico-mg/noticia/sem-previsao-em-votar-balanco-de-2020-at letico-mg-prepara-evento-para-mostrar-realidade-financeira-divida -ultrapassa-r-1-bilhao.ghtml. Accessed March 26, 2021.

Ribeiro, Fred, and Guilherme Frossard. "Jorge Sampaoli Says Goodbye to Atlético-MG," *Globo.com* (February 22, 2021). https://ge.globo .com/futebol/times/atletico-mg/noticia/jorge-sampaoli-se-despede -do-atletico-mg-sigam-caminhando-com-o-coracao-como-guia.g html. Accessed May 6, 2022.

Rodrigues, José Carlos. "Revisitando a malandragem," *ALCEU: Revista de Comunicação, Cultura e Política* 19, no. 37 (2018): 6–15.

"Ronaldinho Thanks Fans for Mother's Tribute," *sportskeeda* (September 24, 2012). https://www.sportskeeda.com/football/ronaldinho -thanks-fans-for-mothers-tribute. Accessed July 13, 2022.

Schudel, Matt. "Dom Phillips, Journalist Who Chronicled Amazon Deforestation, Is Dead at 57," *Washington Post* (June 18, 2022). https://www.washingtonpost.com/obituaries/2022/06/17/dom-phil lips-brazil-dies/. Accessed June 19, 2022.

Silva, Chantal Duarte, and Gustavo Miranda Guimarães. "The Constitution of Brazilian Footballing Speech Objects: Atlético Mineiro Club as a Club of Great Achievements or a Discursive Object Well Built?" *International Journal of Language and Linguistics* 3, no. 5 (November 2016): 81–92.

Silva, Marcelino Rodrigues da. "A cidade dividida nas charges de Mangabeira," *Revista Z* 6 (2010). https://revistazcultural-pacc-ufrj -br.translate.goog/a-cidade-dividida-nas-charges-de-mangabeira-de -marcelino-rodrigues-da-silva/?_x_tr_sch=http&_x_tr_sl=pt& _x_tr_tl=en&_x_tr_hl=en&_x_tr_pto=sc. Accessed May 23, 2022.

———. "Guará, o craque que não foi: Ficção e história na biografia esportiva," *Aletria* 26, no. 3 (2016): 157–174.

———. "A massa faz 100 anos: Futebol e sociedade em BH hoje," *Recorte* 5, no. 2 (2008): 1–5.

———. "O mundo do futebol e a crônica esportiva," *FuLiA* 2, no. 3 (2018): 86–106.

———. "Nas margens do futebol, a literatura (e vice-versa)," *Revista Interfaces* 20, no. 1 (January–June 2014): 15–27.

———. "Quem não gosta de samba . . . não é doente do pé: Carnaval e futebol em Belo Horizonte," *Revista Interfaces* 11 (2008): 83–90.

Skidmore, Thomas E. "Race and Class in Brazil: Historical Perspectives," *Luso-Brazilian Review* 20, no. 1 (Summer 1983): 104–118.

Soares, Antonio Jorge Gonçalves. "Futebol, raça e nacionalidade no Brasil: Releitura da história official" (Doutorado em Educação Fisica, Universidade Gama Filho, Rio de Janeiro, 1998).

Soares, Antonio Jorge, and Hugo Rodolfo Lovisolo. "A construção histórica do estilo nacional," *Revista Brasileira de ciências do esporte* 25, no. 1 (2003): 129–143.

Souto Maior, Eduardo Magalhães. "Impacto da pandemia na quantidade de gols na primeira divisão do Campeonato Brasileiro de Futebol." Trabalho de Conclusão de Curso (Bacharelado em Educação Física— Universidade Federal de Pernambuco, Recife, 2022).

Souza, Eduardo Araripe Pacheco de. "Fazer alianças: Uma escolha determinante entre o protagonismo e a invisibilidade dos grupos organizados de torcedores de futebol no Brasil" (Ph.D. dissertation in Anthropology, Universidade Federal de Pernambuco, 2016).

Souza, Túlio Mayã Ferreira Barros de. "Relação entre estresse e ansiedade no rendimento de atletas de futebol de campo" (Bacharel em Educação Física, Universidade Federal de Pernambuco, Centro Acadêmico de Vitória, 2019).

Thorn, John. "Whitman, Melville, and Baseball: Some Bicentennial Musings," *mlblogs.com* (June 15, 2012). https://ourgame.mlblogs .com/whitman-melville-and-baseball-662f5ef3583d. Accessed June 20, 2022.

Thorpe, Holly, Joshua I. Newman, and David L. Andrews. "Introduction: Assembling COVID/COVID Assemblages," in *Sport and Physical Culture in Global Pandemic Times*, ed. David L. Andrews, Holly Thorpe, and Joshua I. Newman (London: Palgrave Macmillan, 2023), 1–35.

Torres, Luisa Turbino. "The Politics of Being a Soccer Fan: An Ethnographic Perspective on Feminist Activism around Soccer in Brazil" (Ph.D. Dissertation, Political Science and International Relations, University of Delaware, 2022).

"Turco Says It's Difficult to Explain Atlético-MG's Defeat to Fluminense," *Goa Spotlight* (June 2022). https://thegoaspotlight.com/2022/06/09 /turco-says-its-difficult-to-explain-atletico-mgs-defeat-to-flum inense-night-to-forget-athletic-mg/. Accessed June 13, 2022.

Tur-Porcar, Ana, and Domingo Ribeiro-Soriano. "The Role of Emotions and Motivations in Sports Organizations," *Frontiers in Psychology*

11 (October 2020), 12–19. Special issue on "The Management of Emotions in Sports Organizations," ed. Manuel Alonso Dos Santos, Ferran Calabuig Moreno, and Irena Valantine.

Velasco, Franklin, and Rafael Jorda. "Portrait of Boredom among Athletes and Its Implications in Sports Management: A Multi-Method Approach," *Frontiers in Psychology* 11 (October 2020), 29–40.

Vickery, Tim. "Unlike Europe, Brazilian League Preserves Its Competitive Balance," *SportsIllustrated.com* (May 2, 2010). https://www.si.com/more-sports/2010/05/02/brazil. Accessed January 8, 2021.

Wendling, Thierry. *Ethnologie des joueurs d'échecs* (Paris: Presses Universitaires de France, 2002).

Williams, Raymond. *Marxism and Literature* (New York: Oxford University Press, 1977).

Wisnik, José Miguel. *Veneno remédio: O futebol e o Brasil* (São Paulo: Companhia das Letras, 2008).

Young, James. "Ronaldinho's Confounding Mexico Move Likely Motivated by Money," *SportsIllustrated.com* (September 6, 2014). https://www.si.com/soccer/2014/09/06/ronaldinho-queretaro-fc-mexico-brazil-atletico-mineiro. Accessed May 13, 2022.

Zir, Alessandro. "Ontological Excess and Metonymy in Early Modern Descriptions of Brazil: Narratives of the Implausible," *Scripta Uniandrade* 15, no. 1 (2017): 186–204.

Zirin, Dave. *Brazil's Dance with the Devil: The World Cup, the Olympics, and the Fight for Democracy* (Chicago: Haymarket Books, 2014).

Index

Dabus, Marilene, 40–41, 132n31
Dadá Maravilha. *See* Dario
DaMatta, Roberto, 31–32, 93
Dario (Dario José dos Santos), 82–85,
86, 87–88, 141n67
Deliberative Council of the National
Institute for the Development of
Sport, 86
Dias, Rubens Antonio, 111
dictatorship, 94
Didi (Waldyr Pereira), 39, 132n26
Diéz, Ricardo, 99
Dondinho (João Ramos do
Nascimento), 125n20
Drummond, Roberto, 108

Eco, Umberto, 124n10
Éder Aleixo (Éder Aleixo de Assis), 66
Elias, Norbert, 94, 95
Elsey, Brenda, 64
employment contract, 86
Eriksson, Peter, 43
ESPN Brazilian fan blog, 62
evangelical Christians, 53
Éverson, 49

Família e futebol (home movie),
100–102
fan base: amor characteristic, 14–15,
61–62, 65–66, 77–82, 88; attendance levels, 134n41; benefits card,
15, 127n40; Black supporters, 45,
61; call-and-response emotions,
46–47; carnival spirit, 93; collective
personality, 65–66; collective ritual
of football, 127n35; consumers vs.,
2; contagion theory of crowd psychology, 60; crowd culture, 133n39;
demographics of organized supporters, 80, 141n61; ethnic sections of
stadium, 61–62; feelings, 10, 81,
126n30 (*see also* amor; raça); iden-
tification with Galo, 11; network
of connectedness, 95; as "players,"
10–11, 20; raça characteristic,
14–15, 46–52, 56; support during
COVID, 57–58, 60, 94–95; torcida,

45, *45*, 46–47, 79–81, 92, 94–95,
133n39, 142n6; twelfth man, 46
Fanon, Frantz, 35
Farred, Grant, 38
fascism, 94
FC Barcelona (club), 106
Fédération Internationale de Football
Association (FIFA), 104, 144n27,
145n49
feelings. *See* fan base; players
Fernández, Nacho, 51
Ferreira, João, 37
Ferreira, Rivaldo Vítor Borba, 53
FIFA, 104, 144n27, 145n49
fighting, correspondence between
amor and playing, 66–77
Filho, Jair Ventura, 41
Filho, Mario, 36–37
fist, symbol of upraised, 41–42, *42*
Fiuza, Luciana, 24, 43
Flamengo (club): anthem, 133n38;
CAM's loss in league championship, 80; CAM vs., 51; competition
with CAM, 6; Copa do Brasil,
72–73; Copa Libertadores, 50,
66, 69, 70–71, 81, 138n22; defeat
of Bangu, 2; mascot, 11; Union
of Great Brazilian Football Clubs
founder, 129n54
Fluminense (club), 48, 49, 107,
129n54, 132nn28–31
Flusser, Vilém, 126n27
football: academics' treatment of,
95–97; branding/image, 88; Brazil's
self-image as emotional involvement in football, 82; cartel of
club owners, 9, 126n24; collective
ritual, 127n35; competitive effort
vs. licensed violence, 8–9, 39–40;
contact sport, 9; diversity and inclusion, 76; draw (tie) ending, 46, 49,
50; employment contract, 86; enthusiasm for, 1, 2, 123n3; experience
from stadium seat, 47–48; Freud
on, 59–60, 72, 136n4; generational
impact, 70; homophobia, 62; impact
of infectious diseases, 8; interna-

170 \ Index

Recopa Sudamericana, 6, 106
Reinaldo (José Reinaldo de Lima; O
    Rei), 18, 24, 41–46, 69, 102–103,
    129n50, 137n8
Reis, Afonso Celso Garcia, 109,
    145n45
religion, 52–54
Resistência, 45. *See also* fan base
Réver (Réver Humberto Alves de
    Araújo), 56–58
Rio de Janeiro, Brazil, 3, 8
Rivaldo (Rivaldo Vítor Borba
    Ferreira), 53
Robinho (Robson de Souza), 64–65,
    135n54, 137n14
Rodrigues, Nelson, 136n4
Rolling Stones, 51
Ronaldinho Gaúcho (Ronaldo de Assis
    Moreira), 104–107, *104*, 137n8
the Rooster. *See* Galo
Rosa, João Guimarães, 97
Rousseff, Dilma, 17
rowing, 38
Rubens (Rubens Antonio Dias), 111

Said (Said Paulo Arges), 77
salary. *See* players, wages
Sampaio, Luiz Sérgio Coelho de, 96
Sampaoli, Jorge, 7, 12, 125n18
Santana, Telê, 54
Santos (club), 6, 11, 46–50, 129n54
Santos, Dario José dos. *See* Dario
Santos, Manuel Francisco dos, 37
Santos, Neymar da Silva, Jr., 53,
    135n54
São Paulo, Brazil, 3
São Paulo FC (club), 6, 18, 46–50, 81,
    92, 129n54
SARS-CoV-2 coronavirus. *See*
    COVID-19
Sávio, Eugênio, 111, 112
Schalke 04 (club), 97
Schechtel, Luiz Eduardo, 19
Schiller, Friedrich, 138n27
The Selects (Seleção; Brazilian nation-
    al team), 29
sexism in football, 62–66

sexual violence, 64–66, 137n14
Shankly, Bill, 140n45
Silva, João Alves de Assis, 137n8
Silva, Luiz Inácio Lula da, 91, 130n11
Silva, Marcelino Rodrigues da, 24,
    123n5, 124nn10–12
skin whitening, 40–41, 132n31
slavery, 35
Smith, Tommie, 41
Soares, Alice Quintão, 62–65, 81
Soares, Antonio, 131n19
soccer. *See* football
Social Democrats, 84
Sousa, Givanildo Vieira de, 20
South American Championship of
    Nations (Sul Americano), 8,
    126n22
Souza, Allan Rodrigues de, 20
Souza, Robson de, 64–65, 135n54,
    137n14
sports and games. *See* play
sports chronicle, 124n12
Sports Illustrated, 105
Stade Français (club), 99
Stein, Gertrude, 52, 135n51
Stellantis automotive group, 75–76,
    140n53
Stival, Alexi. *See* Cuca
supporters. *See* fan base

Theory of Human Editions, 48–49
Thorpe, Holly, 4
ticket prices, 134n41
Tilico, Mário, 40
titulares, 6, 125n17
Torcida Organizada Dragões da
    F.A.O., 15. *See also* fan base
Torres, Carlos Alberto, 132n31
Tournament of Champions, 5

Ubaldo (Ubaldo Miranda), 99
Ubirajara (Ubirajara Gonçalves
    Motta), 41
Unidade Popular (UP), 94
Union of Great Brazilian Football
    Clubs, 19, 129n54
UP (Unidade Popular), 94

David Faflik is Professor of English at the University of Rhode Island. He is the author of *Boarding Out: Inhabiting the American Urban Literary Imagination, 1840–1860*; *Melville and the Question of Meaning*; *Urban Formalism: The Work of City Reading*; *Transcendental Heresies: Harvard and the Modern American Practice of Unbelief*; and *The Literary Gift in Early America*.

www.ingramcontent.com/pod-product-compliance
Lightning Source LLC
Chambersburg PA
CBHW020612270326
41927CB00005B/297